D0881713

BEST CANADIAN ESSAYS 2015

Best Canadian Essays 2015

Edited by

Christopher Doda

and

David Layton

TIGHTROPE BOOKS

Tightrope Books
#207-2 College St
Toronto ON M5G 1K3
www.tightropebooks.com

SERIES EDITOR: Christopher Doda
GUEST EDITOR: David Layton
MANAGING EDITOR: Heather Wood
PROOFREADING: Natalie Fuerth
COVER DESIGN: Deanna Janovski
TYPOGRAPHY: Kris Westerlaken

We thank the Canada Council for the Arts and the Ontario Arts Council
for their support of our publishing program.

PRINTED AND BOUND IN CANADA

A cataloguing record for this publication is available from Library and
Archives Canada

Contents

Preface

SOME TIME AGO I spent five years as the Submissions Editor for one of Canada's esteemed literary journals. Almost entirely short fiction and poetry, the work I received was, in general, by aspiring or unknown (to me anyway) writers. I mention this detail because it pointed to what would-be writers were looking at for their early topics and source material. The poetry was pretty much a grab-bag but I noticed after a time that short stories had a tendency to arrive in bunches. A certain subject matter would be disproportionately represented for one or two months and then fade away. I had groups about everything from vampires or elves (something I found odd as the journal was not known *at all* for fantasy writing) to yoga to ESL teaching overseas to stories about failed writers.

In this, my fifth year as Series Editor for *Best Canadian Essays*, I have noticed a similar tendency as I read journals and magazines from across the country. When I started there was a lot of writing about the (supposed) end to the wars in Iraq and Afghanistan. Another year, there were many pieces about coping with mental illness. I've encountered a lot of memoirs about caring for an elderly/sick/demented/all of the above parent, or reminiscences about the recently deceased all of the above parent (represented here in Kathleen Kennedy's wrenching "Remember This"). One year, there was a lot of interest in environmental degradation, usually focussed on the Alberta tar sands. In another, much was said about animal rights. Recently, muzzling of scientists and increased government secrecy are hot-button topics. And, not surprisingly, Canada's numerous literary journals annually contain many essays about art and literature (such as Darryl Whetter's look at the uneasy relationship between English academia and creative writing itself, "Can't Lit," found at the close of this book).

So welcome to the Law and Order volume of *Best Canadian Essays*. As David Layton and I prepared our final list of contributors, I noticed that a full seven out of fifteen, nearly half, in some way concern themselves with law enforcement and the legal system. Mary Rogan's "The Killing of Sammy Yatin," which details the police shooting death of a mentally ill teenager on a Toronto streetcar and John Lorinc's chilling look at how urban police forces are becoming more militaristic, both in weaponry and outlook, "Armed and Dangerous," (cover stories in their respective magazines) outline the potential for abuse of power. Sinéad Mulhern writes about the life of a female prison inmate in "Crime and Punishment." Somewhat tangentially, Paul Haarvardsrud exposes how the Alberta government uses slippery interpretations of FOI legislation to withhold publically held information from its own citizenry in "Access Denied" (though this problem is hardly unique to Alberta—see note on government secrecy above). On the foreign front, Tanya Bellehumeur-Allat's "Beirut Bombing" shows us the life of a young woman in a city under virtual martial law and Jason O'Hara has a violent run-in with Rio de Janeiro's notoriously brutal police force in the lead-up to the 2014 FIFA World Cup (another cover story). Finally Naheed Mustafa sheds light on the coordinated police investigation that lead to the arrest of two men who plotted to derail a VIA train outside Toronto. An exposé of the law and those most affected by it wasn't intentional on our part but, rather, points to something happening in the zeitgeist, a trend that shows no hint of slowing as the volume of writing on the subject certainly outweighs the 'best' included here.

Of course, the 2015 edition of *Best Canadian Essays* is not all doom and gloom. Greg Hudson humorously confronts his physical transience at the age of 30 (!) when his body's physiological processes are scientifically mapped as much older in "Hope I'm Old Before I Die." Jessamyn Hope also ponders mortality as she contemplates a potentially fatal high dive in "The Reverse" under the glaring watch of her coach. The human capacity to maintain cherished beliefs in the face of overwhelming evidence to the contrary gets Eve Corbel thinking about herself in "Getting It Wrong." Timothy Taylor even learns to *appreciate* taxes in "Happy Returns." In "Ol' Talk," Nadine Bachan considers her relation to the accent and speech of her Trinidadian family. And Adam Gopnik's "Expos Nation" is nominally an article about Montreal's former baseball team but is really an ode to his childhood city and time spent with his father.

I imagine that the current issues that dominate the headlines now will inspire next year's volume of *Best Canadian Essays* simply because they represent the topics that people most want to talk about at this time. Whether it's the federal election (or issues raised during the election like oil pipeline development, the treatment of the Aboriginal population, the aging Baby Boomer demographic, the income gap, the shrinking of the middle class, burdens on the health care system, the economy in general etc.), the refugee crisis in Syria, the vaccine debate, the ongoing effects of globalization, efforts to contain deadly viruses, or how these and other matters impact people on a more personal level, I expect to be reading about them in the coming year. And I expect that Canadians will write about them with their usual foresight, thoughtfulness, acumen and punctiliousness, and with their usual forthright style.

— *Christopher Doda*

Introduction

What is the origin of the essay? Michel de Montaigne is largely credited with creating and naming this form of non-fiction writing in the 16th century. From a historical perspective, we might go further back in time to the literature of ancient Greece and Rome from which Montaigne received his inspiration, and then forward again to the Enlightenment and the rise of the political polemicist. Still following history's arrow, we might examine how the growth of urbanization, literacy rates and economic prosperity brought forth a new and vibrant market for literary production until finally we reach the bullseye of our present moment, where the full flowering—or eminent destruction—of the essay form will be wrought by the rise of the Internet and social media.

But what if the question is asked in a more limited and personal way? What is the origin—the motivation—for picking up the proverbial pen and committing one's thoughts to paper? The current literary situation in Canada certainly eliminates any notion that one is doing it for the money. It's also never been entirely clear what, exactly, constitutes an essay. Montaigne himself was famously circumspect about offering a definition.

From the experience of living in Lebanon during the civil

war in Tanya Bellehumeur-Allatt's "Beirut Bombing" to the fear of high-jump diving in Jessamyn Hope's "The Reverse" to the militarization of our police in John Lorinc's "Armed and Dangerous," this year's superb Canadian collection will attest that essays can be political, personal, polemical, passionately persuasive or plaintive. So what, if anything, binds them together?

Without any wish to cause offense and provoke what perhaps would be justified denials from this year's contributors, I'd like to suggest that the creative origin of the essay rests with the lowly, and highly misunderstood, rant. Essayists aren't ranters, but often essays begin life as rants. The rant is not some distant cousin of the essay, the kind that is kept in the attic when the other family members arrive for dinner. Rather, a rant is the caterpillar to the essay's butterfly. Not only are they intimately linked but one repeatedly follows from the other.

As this year's editor for *Best Canadian Essays* let me avoid any appearance of conflict of interest by stating up front that I am a ranter. Many people tell me that I am, so I must bow to public opinion. I have no interest in using this forum to offer a mere defense of my own behaviour, but I have often wondered what the animating principle is behind a good (or bad) rant. Why do we rant and what might it have in common with the essay?

There is certainly something obsessive about a rant, because ranters, even if jumping from topic to topic, are recognizably focussed on one particular subject. They might go on (and on) about government, bad parenting or rental car agencies, but the true origin of their ire, no matter how misplaced, is an underlying sense of injustice. Something is wrong with the world and ranters want you to know what it is. They *need* you to know about it because they themselves can't stop ruminating, worrying and returning to what amounts to an intellectual itch that, no matter how many times it is scratched, returns to torment them over and over again.

Is it any wonder that ranters end up talking loudly and with frequent anger? Or that their excessive complaints are perceived to be unreasonable? Rants are bombastic and repetitive. They are also boring. In other words, everything an essay is not. "When you stay in your room and rage or sneer or shrug your shoulders, as I did for many years, the world and its problems are impossibly daunting," says writer and essayist Jonathan Franzen. If a rant is an embryonic essay, an essay is nevertheless almost an anti-rant because it depends on eloquence, elegance and a tone of deft reasonableness. Even though it still wishes to be persuasive, there's that pressing need to be heard, to make a point, and if you listen closely you can hear the author's animating sense of justice pulsing through the work. "Whatever I most hated, at a particular moment, became the thing I wanted to write about," says Franzen, and whether that's true or not for most essayists, and specifically those selected here, what's most interesting is the transmuting effect Franzen claims has had such a deep influence on his outlook. The real danger, he suggests, is that you might end up loving, or at least arriving at a deeper understanding of, your opponent. This is not to suggest that the underlying goal of an essay is to eventually love thy neighbour, or even necessarily to embrace him or her, but that the tone, which should never be shrill or strident, should approach its subject with a measured intensity.

In Greg Hudson's hilarious "Before I Die" the enemy is the author's too rapidly aging mind and body. Visiting an "age management clinic" Hudson discovers that though chronologically he might be a newly minted 30, "My skin is 11 years older than me; my immune system is 52 years old, and I have the telomeres of a 49-year-old." Angry but hopeful, his answer to such unsettling news is to start running and lose weight, a form of punishment he consciously unleashes against his body for "aging too soon." Darryl Whetter's wonderfully titled "Can't Lit" explores how English departments impede creative writing in Canada. Spending two years as the coordinator of a creative writing program at a major university, Whetter discovers the unacceptable fact that "writing in Canada is managed (and sometimes even taught) by professors who have never published creative writing." Such departments and individuals seem in many cases hostile to the emotional complexity that underlines all good writing, a point he strengthens by offering, as a rebuttal, an exceptionally well-written essay. Staying on the topic of writing and words, Nadine Bachan's "Ol' Talk" offers a wonderful account of how reading VS Naipaul reignited her passion for her native Trinidadian dialect. Growing up in Canada, Bachan says that she has "always been conscious of the way I speak, hyper-aware of the sounds that fight to be the first out of my mouth." That it took Naipaul, the Nobel Prize winning author who left—'escaped' would more likely be the word he would use—Trinidad at 18 and who speaks with a self-consciously adopted Oxford accent, to regain an appreciation of Trinidadian speech is part of the irony that intelligently infuses her story. People, like dialects, are hard to pin down and catalogue.

This perhaps is the age of rant. For proof, look no further than Donald Trump. When everyone can have their say it can be argued that nobody except those who bark the loudest ever get heard. Yet rather than bemoan the fact, maybe it's best to think of every blog and comment page as cocoons ready to emerge as multi-coloured butterflies. This year's superb collection of Canadian essays certainly—and hopefully—points in that direction.

— *David Layton*

BEST CANADIAN ESSAYS 2015

Ol' Talk

NADINE BACHAN

"DIS BOI WILL eat up he family in trut."

I read the line aloud with its Trinidadian inflections, in the way I believed the character would have actually spoken it. The words—uttered with unease by the protagonist's father in VS Naipaul's novel *A House for Mr. Biswas*—flowed out of me, and it felt good. Better than good. It had been a very long time since I'd last sat alone and felt compelled to use dialect. Like a comforting scent, the lyrical highs and lows triggered familiar feelings both warm and conflicted, much more complicated than nostalgia.

In the novel, this line, along with all of the dialogue, is written in British English: "This boy will eat up his family in truth."

I WAS A SEEN-AND-NOT-HEARD child. Raised to be polite and tight-lipped, my meekness allowed my presence among adults to go mostly unnoticed. Always within earshot of lively conversation—fast-talking, grin-inducing and punctuated with laughter—I took in all the unfiltered chatter.

When I was six years old, I was at one of the countless house parties my family was invited to in the early years of our new life in Canada. We revelled in our own little social village then, made up mostly of relatives and close friends

3

who were also recent immigrants from Trinidad. There was always some birthday or milestone celebration, or holiday get-together, or just-because-we-deserve-a-bit-of-fun fête to attend.

A man in the crowd began to look around the room, trying to locate his wife. He asked the people nearest to him if they had seen her. I could have asked, "Where is she?" but a choice phrase came to my mind, something I had heard earlier and logged away as one of those fun little idioms. I yelled out: "Whey she dey dey?"

Several people around me laughed, loudly. I delighted in the attention until I saw my mother's face. Her smile was pursed and forced. Her eyes stared down at me in that tell-tale way. I'd done something wrong. She took me by the hand, led me aside and reprimanded me to tears.

In Trinidad, *Whey she dey dey?* scrapes the bottom of the inevitable hierarchy of speech that exists in any language. Saying the phrase at my tender age was akin to a toddler blurting out an expletive after stubbing a toe. I hadn't cussed, but my mother corrected me as if I had; what I had said was improper, coarse, foul—I was never to speak that way again.

From then on, I did as children do when they want to learn how to navigate the world: I followed the cues of my parents. I listened with a turned ear whenever they spoke to Canadians. Although my parents' Trinidadian accents were never fully erased, their diction and tone would shift to something deliberate, with much of the colour wrung out.

I have always been conscious of the way I speak, hyper-aware of the sounds that fight to be the first out of my mouth. My group classroom portraits when I was young were quintessentially multicultural—rows upon rows of toothy, chubby-cheeked faces of nearly every ethnicity a person could imagine. However, most of my young school-mates were born and raised in Canada and spoke with Canadian accents like all of my teachers. Before I understood what the word meant, assimilation was my goal.

While my accent is now dominantly Canadian, there are still occasions when I speak in slang, with a somewhat garbled and uneven Caribbean articulation. I'm prone to over-think and over-enunciate, worried that I'm saying things wrong. Whatever "wrong" is. Attempting to reconcile the polarity of being a Trinidadian-Canadian—and the tug-of-war of allegiances that goes with the attempt—is an exercise in self-discovery that has been both enriching and exhaustingly circular.

NATURE DRIVES US to adjust to our circumstances. The mimic octopus will twist and turn and fold its body to look like various kinds of fish, or snakes, or to simply disappear into the sea bed. The lyrebird will reproduce the sounds of its environment, including the mating call of other birds and animals. Assimilation may begin as a survival tactic of sorts, but it's also a matter of choice. And unlike my animal comrades, I get to be cognitively conflicted about what I do and why.

The intricacy of verbal indicators—language, word choice, even something as simple as an upward inflection—can speak volumes about a person. Hearing a familiar accent or a hometown turn-of-phrase in public is like detecting a homing beacon. Everything else fades into white noise. "Language is such an emotional issue for everyone," says Molly Babel, an aptly named professor of linguistics at the University of British Columbia (UBC) who focuses on speech perception in societies with a range of dialects. "It is a huge part of our presentation of our identities and others use it—for better or worse—to label and categorize us."

The biggest misconception, Babel says, is probably "that some dialects or accents are better than others." She cites the North American perception that a British accent sounds intelligent and elegant, while an accent from the southern United States sounds unsophisticated. "In a nutshell, we are more likely to imitate the speech patterns of others when we have positive feelings towards that individual or what that individual's speech patterns represent." On the other hand, linguistic discrimination is the act of prejudice against a person because of the way they speak. It's wrapped up in the notion that speech indicates upbringing, education, economic status, prestige, sociocultural environment and a plethora of other factors that serve to maintain an audible pecking order. Dialect is interpreted as a barometer of strength and weakness. Of intelligence and stupidity. George Orwell called it being "branded on the tongue."

When I was still a child, one of my cousins was forced to enrol in speech therapy, the elementary school's attempt to fix how he spoke. While his mother was earning her master's degree in Guelph, Ontario, he lived with my family in the Etobicoke suburbs of Toronto and enrolled in school with me and my siblings. He was diagnosed with a long list of "problematic" speech patterns that were really nothing more than a Trinidadian accent. He didn't pronounce the *th* at the beginnings of words. Thing was *ting*. The was *dee*. Them was *dem*. He also didn't pronounce the *er* at the end of words. Water was *wat-ah*. Teacher was *teach-ah*.

He attended therapy diligently, but the vocal exercises didn't stick. He pronounced all of the words exactly as he was instructed, then walked out of the room and immediately fell back into his natural way of speaking. In the end, it didn't matter. Although it had been their initial plan to stay in Canada, my aunt and cousin decided they ought to return to Trinidad. From time to time, my cousin will talk about how much he disliked going to those sessions. To this day, whenever I speak to him, he affects an exaggerated Canadian accent to tease me: "How's the weather up there in Cana-*der*?" I suspect the voice he employs is that of his former speech therapist.

My cousin would be pleased to learn that in her forty-plus-year career, Barbara May Bernhardt—a clinical speech pathologist who teaches at UBC's School of Audiology and Speech Sciences—has seen a significant turnaround in how speech-language pathologists approach accent reduction. "Pronunciation-wise, there are often misconceptions when considering speech without dialect. It can be sometimes misconstrued as 'development errors,' which would be an incorrect assessment when a person's cultural upbringing is not considered." Misdiagnosing dialect as language difficulty or impairment can result in detrimental long-term effects, including feelings of low self-worth and negative attitudes towards education.

Unlike the lessons experienced by my cousin, the British Columbia school system's practices incorporate a "bidialectal" approach, which respects both the standard and the dialect. Standard English as a Second Language is a linguistic phenomenon that is now recognized in schools in indigenous communities in the province. One of the core beliefs of the American Speech-Language-Hearing Association is that no dialectal variety of American English is a disorder or a pathological form of speech or language. And, all across the globe, variants of World English (also known as International English, which includes dialects of all forms) are becoming more prevalent and accepted.

However, both Babel and Bernhardt acknowledge that

discrimination based on voice still exists. The first impression when interviewing for a job or meeting new colleagues is so important to professional development and is influenced by several factors, including how we speak. Because of this, some adults opt for accent reduction therapy.

I USED TO describe the way my parents and most of my relatives spoke as broken English. I had heard more than a few people use the term during my childhood. For years, no one corrected me. I was eventually told by my sister, who was enthusiastically contemplating all manner of things in her undergraduate studies at the time, that the language Trinidadians speak is not broken English but, rather, a dialect.

Some would argue that there isn't much of a difference between language and dialect. Max Weinreich, a Yiddish sociolinguist, popularized the saying, "A language is a dialect with an army and a navy." As the writer Lauren Webb asks, "Why is it that one language is classed as a language, and another is classed a dialect? Some dialects have hundreds of thousands of speakers, whereas some languages have less than one thousand." But my feeling that Trinidadian English was somehow *lesser* than the Queen's English continued to plague me for many years.

My mother and father both speak in a dialect associated with the southern region of Trinidad, comprised mostly of small towns and farming communities. Their accent indicates a middle- or working-class background. The difference is subtle, but makes for an emphatic social marker that separates most of my family from those who live north, in and near the capital city Port of Spain, a region associated with upper-class sensibilities.

My aunt has lived in southern Trinidad her entire life. She and I share a quietness; we are listeners in a very vocal family. Her childhood stories are seldom told, which invests anything she tells me with added resonance.

As a scrappy ten-year-old, my aunt once ran through her father's garden in bare feet and stepped on a thorn. She hobbled inside, yelling:

"Someting jook my foot!"

At the time, one of her own aunts (my great-aunt or Tanty) had been entertaining a suitor. They were enjoying an afternoon tea on my grandmother's Royal Doulton, the china set she kept on the highest shelf in her living room display case. The suitor—a wealthy man from a gated community in the north—turned to my aunt and said, "Say that again."

She repeated herself. "Someting jook me."

He smirked at her. "Now, I don't think that's the right word. Do you?"

She was confused. She had no idea what he was talking about.

He continued, "Jook. Jook is not correct. What is the proper word?"

He spoke the word "jook" as though it was a bad taste in his mouth and made her stand in the middle of the room, waiting while she grew mortified and close to tears. After several minutes of silence, he finally let her off the hook.

"The correct word is jab. Or prick," he said before waving her away.

Prick, indeed.

BY THE TIME I was a teenager—engulfed by the turmoil of finding my footing in high school—my Canadian accent became my dominant voice, both in public and at home. However, I had the ability to "turn off" the Canadian and "turn on" the Trinidadian when the situation called for it.

Sometimes, my classmates would ask me to "say something in Trini." I always shrank at the thought and they always urged me on. I would close my eyes and feel the stretch of my embarrassed grin, uncomfortable on the centre stage. They'd give me a sentence to convert and I'd do it for them like I was performing a party trick.

Eventually, I refused to flaunt my Trinidadian accent for kicks with friends. It felt degrading. I was tired of being pointed out for what made me different and politely denied the requests until I simply lost the ability to "turn it on." I couldn't switch to the Trinidadian dialect outside of my home anymore, and that was fine by me. By then, I had been living in Canada for fifteen years, and I was feeling all that much closer to being a true citizen of the Great White North.

My connection to dialect now exists predominantly in the speech of others, but I fall into that way of speaking whenever I'm in the presence of close company. A word here or there will flourish at the end when I chat with my mother and father, or I might use a certain expression to make a point when conversing with my brother and sister. Speaking to each other in this subtly fluctuating way is just one facet of our family's intimacy. Still, whatever the occasion may be, I would always become aware of the shift and it never sounded right. I had come to terms with the fact that I had lost the ability to enjoy speaking in my dialect until I began to read *A House for Mr. Biswas*.

The Trinidadian opinion of VS Naipaul is fascinating. Although he was born and raised in Trinidad, he moved to England at the age of eighteen. The novel has been perceived as a fictional re-telling of Naipaul's father's life, based on the writer's childhood memories. Mohun, the protagonist, steers away from expectations dictated by generations of deeply-rooted tradition; his is a lifelong struggle with "culture," trying to be his own man. The book earned Naipaul international acclaim and established him as one of the best writers of his time. Despite this success, there is a sizable group of Trinidadians who call him a traitor, a man who left the country only to exploit it years later for literary fame. He has been judged for misrepresenting the land and its people. While there are many reasons for the contempt—Naipaul is notoriously thorny and unaccommodating—his careful Oxbridge accent is one very noticeable indication of his distance from his birthplace.

An incident supposedly occurred several years ago during one of Naipaul's visits to Trinidad, not long after he received the Nobel Prize. It's a story that has made its rounds viva voce, certainly shifting and evolving as it passes from mouth to mouth. A large crowd had gathered at an event to celebrate the author's literary work and achievements. Several people asked him questions about his writing, his inspiration and his life in England. One frowning man stood up and, in a very strong accent, said simply, "I knew your father." Four words meant to pull him down, to remind him that he had come from humble beginnings. Four words meant to *jook* what some have deemed an inflated ego.

Naipaul made his choice very firmly and relatively simply: he would become an English gentleman and leave Trinidad mostly behind. For many of us, it's not so easy. Jodi Picoult wrote it best in *Change of Heart*: "In the space between yes and no, there's a lifetime. It's the difference between the path you walk and the one you leave behind; it's the gap between who you thought you could be and who you really are."

During one of our cross-country video-chats, I tell my parents that I'm finally reading the Naipaul novel. We discuss the beauty of the book's narrative and language and my father's face lights up, as it always does when he tells me about his youth. His words are rich with cherished memory. He smiles inwardly at things I will never fully understand.

For a long time, I was envious that I didn't have that same strong connection to the place where I was born. Yet, somehow, it feels much more precious, seeing those people and places entirely through his telling—through his voice.

Beirut Bombing

TANYA BELLEHUMEUR-ALLATT

In Lebanon, nothing is surprising ...
—Israeli Foreign Minister Yitzhak Shamir, April 1983

IN THE THREE months since our arrival in Beirut, we'd never gone out after dark. Around five, soon after the muezzin's call to prayer, the shelling would begin. We could always hear it, even when it came from behind the mountains. At dusk we would pull the heavy drapes across all our apartment windows—"We wouldn't want anyone to see inside," Maman liked to say, but I knew the real reason—as if *they* could protect us from the terrors of the night.

Still, I had to ask: "Maman, there's a Sadie Hawkins dance at school next Friday night." We were washing the supper dishes by candlelight in our apartment kitchen. Blackouts in the city were frequent.

"You're not going." She grabbed the frying pan with her gloved hands and leaned her weight into the sink to scrub.

"Please, Maman, everyone will be there. Can't you make an exception? Just this once?" My glasses were steaming up from the boiling water she'd just added to the sink. The city's septic system had mixed with the fresh water supply, and we needed to add ammonia or bleach to our bathing and washing water. The sharp, aggressive smell of the disinfectant made my eyes water. I turned my back to the sink to escape the odour and wait for my glasses to clear.

It was lonely for us, this business of staying inside, respecting the curfew. Each morning my brother and I walked across the city to attend the American Community School of Beirut, on the campus of the American University of Beirut near the embassy. It was an hour-long walk from our apartment block on the Muslim side of West Beirut to the main streets of the French sector. We always followed the same route, drawn out for us by our father on a map of the city issued by the United Nations.

"Never deviate from this route," he'd warned us, when he'd first shown us the way. The halfway point of the walk was a bombed-out car parked half on the sidewalk, half on the street. Its body was rusted, with all of its available parts removed, but the hollow shell remained, a reminder of the devastation of civil war that had ravaged the city for the last twelve years.

"Keep your heads down. Talk to no one," my father had advised. "Don't stop to look at anything. Maman will worry if you're not home by four."

Our school was in a compound surrounded by a tall iron gate with two guards at the entrance. Each morning we had to show them our identity cards with the school logo and our picture. Then the guards searched our schoolbags, even our lunches, and looked at us hard, as if we were potential criminals. But once we were inside the gate, the scary-looking guards outside made it feel like a safe place.

"What are they looking for?" I'd asked my father at suppertime, a few days after we'd started at the school.

"Explosives," he said. "Weapons. Information. Smuggled goods."

"On me?"

"You might not be who you say you are," he said, lifting his wine glass. "To them, everyone's a suspect."

Whenever his connections in the CIA and the Lebanese militia gave him inside information about what he called 'hot spots' in the city, where violence was expected to erupt, he kept us home from school. It was his job to discover where the fighting would be, and then go there, as a United Nations presence, to bring peace.

But all I could think about was the dance.

"Ginny said her father can come get us after the dance."

"The American helicopter pilot?" my mother asked.

"I could sleep over at their place." I held my breath. My mother splashed more boiling water into the sink. I peeked back at her. Beads of sweat dripped down from her forehead into the water.

"It's not safe. Foreigners get kidnapped at night. All kinds of things could happen."

"Maman, please. One night. Just this once. Everyone is going."

My mother paused. She wiped her face with the back of her gloved hand. "I know it's been hard for you here." She handed me the gleaming frying pan and reached for a stainless steel pot.

"I'll call you as soon as we get to Ginny's."

"What if the phone lines are down?"

It would often take us twenty-five attempts before making a connection. Even then, our conversations could be cut mid-sentence.

"Please, Maman."

She shook her head. "I have to talk to your father. I can't promise you anything. I'm sorry."

"Can we at least go to Groovy's?" It was a European fashion boutique we'd found when we'd first scouted out the downtown.

My mother turned to look at me. In the candlelight, her pupils were big and round, her face soft.

"It's my first high school dance," I said.

"I know."

"I saw a purple miniskirt in the window last time we were on Hamra Street."

"*On verra*," she said, "we'll see."

THE NEXT DAY was Saturday. We sat across from each other at a small round table in a pastry shop in downtown Beirut. "This place reminds me of *la rue Sainte-Catherine*, in Montreal," my mother said. She smoothed the linen tablecloth with her hand. "*Deux chocolatines, s'il vous plaît,*" she called to the pastry chef who doubled as waiter. We watched him use silver tongs to extract two croissants from the display case. "I love all these Old World details, all these *gâteries*," she said.

"*Apportez-moi votre meilleur thé,*" she added, when he placed the pastries before us.

I held the bag from Groovy's in my lap. My mother had agreed to the skirt and even suggested I buy stockings to match. I was relieved and elated that she understood the importance of the outfit—how everything hinged on fitting in.

She sipped her tea from a tiny porcelain cup without handles. "In the gardens of Sri Lanka," she said, "only virgin girls are allowed to harvest the white tea blossoms used to make this tea. They use golden scissors and golden bowls." She held her teacup with both hands in front of her like a sacred object. "To this day, they continue the same practices as they did in the time of the aristocracy, when white tea was reserved for Chinese royalty. Imagine that," she said, bringing her cup to her lips and resting it there. "I am drinking what an oriental empress would drink in the morning, in her private chambers. Does that link my destiny with hers, somehow?"

I looked quizzically at her face, then down at the straw sticking out of my Coke can. "If the fighting gets worse, are we going home?" I asked her.

"Where is home?" she asked, staring into her teacup.

"Canada." How could she not know that? I had an instant stomach ache.

"It's a big country." She pressed the fingers of her right hand down onto her plate to pick up the leftover croissant crumbs. "We're not going back to Yellowknife, if that's what you mean." She licked her fingers slowly, one at a time. I had never seen her do that in public.

"We can stay at Grandmaman's. Anywhere is better than here," I said, pointing out the window with my chin. An old Mercedes taxi, its passenger door held together with duct tape, honked its horn at a group of men in army fatigues. Their machine guns and ammunition belts bounced against their chests as they ran across the street. The car screeched to a halt to let them pass, then charged forward, muffler roaring. In Israel, earlier that year, I'd grown accustomed to seeing armed soldiers on the city streets. The difference here was that there was a war raging a few neighbourhoods over, where the Green Line divided the city into East and West. My father had told us about kidnappings and daily sniping against Lebanese civilians in Christian East Beirut. The UN presence was meant to stop the fighting. Sometimes it did, my father said, and sometimes it didn't.

"We're staying until your father is finished his work," my mother said into the teacup.

I had never seen this side of my mother before: vulnerable, unsure of herself. Until now she'd always been right there alongside my father, ready to follow him on his next adventure. But things were different here. The city was falling down around us.

I thought of how my fourteen-year-old brother had his own passport, with his picture and date of birth, but I didn't. My name and photo were fixed to a page in my mother's passport, as if I were an extension of her, and not my own person. This practice, seemingly unique to Canadians, routinely caused all kinds of complications with Middle Eastern border guards who demanded to know why I didn't have my own documents. In their eyes I was old enough to be married. In my mother's eyes I was an appendage, fully dependent. Where she went, I went. If she fell apart, so would I. It was a terrifying thought.

I sucked on my straw until it made a loud slurping sound. My mother made a face at me and reached for her purse. "Let's head back," she said.

As soon as we got home, I laid my new outfit on the bed for closer inspection. It was perfect. Short purple skirt gathered at the waist, striped stockings that made my legs look funky and long. It was artsy and sophisticated, and I loved it. I thought Richie, the Australian boy in grade eight, would like it too.

I brought the cotton skirt and stockings up to my nose and breathed in the cloying chemical smell of new clothes, then stretched out on my bed and turned my thoughts to Richie.

"I can see your bra through the back of your shirt," he had whispered to me under the big tree in the school compound the day before. It was the only mature tree in our part of the city. All the other ones had been cut down or ruined by the war. I liked leaning against the huge trunk and looking up at the sky through its branches.

"You're sexy," Richie continued.

My face, neck and arms pulsed with instant heat. I hadn't realized my shirt was transparent at the back. Why hadn't Maman told me before I'd left the apartment that morning? Hadn't she noticed?

"You remind me of Brooke Shields in *The Blue Lagoon*." Richie leaned his arm on the trunk of the tree behind me, and brought his face close to mine. I could smell the sweat on his skin.

I turned to look at the kids walking by on their way to class. A few stared. I wondered vaguely if my brother could see me, or if they'd report to him what his sister was up to under the big tree. But then the bell rang, announcing the beginning of classes, and I was saved from Richie's hot breath too close to my neck.

AT SCHOOL THAT Monday, I sat in the library after lunch. My grade seven class was in the basement, for band practice, but I had a free period. Since I'd only started at the school in January, and didn't play a band instrument, I was exempted from music class. I spent my free time on the top floor in the reading lounge, next to Mr. Thierry's classroom. After that, I would study advanced French while my class did beginner, baby French in our regular classroom downstairs. At dinnertime at home, I took perverse pleasure in imitating the way they counted to ten with their thick accents.

Suddenly there was a deafening boom, a sound louder than I'd ever heard before. Everything shook. The room went black. Books fell off the shelves. The chairs next to me rolled over. A window cracked and split, sending shards flying.

After the huge sound of the blast, there was a thick quiet. I sat alone in the darkened library, assessing the damage around me. What just happened? Was it an earthquake? What should I do?

A light shone around me. "*C'est l'heure du français,*" Monsieur Thierry announced when I stood up, eyes blinking, and followed his flashlight beam into the classroom adjacent to the library. For the next hour, we conjugated French verbs by candlelight.

"*Que je puisse, que tu puisses.*" Monsieur Thierry's lips pushed forward when he spoke, as if all the words were teetering on the edge of his mouth, ready to dribble out. I thought of Richie and how '*puisse*' sounded like the English word 'kiss.'

Whether Monsieur Thierry had forgotten about the blast that had just shaken our school, or decided that his curriculum was more important, we carried on covering the board with our white-chalked declensions made visible by the candles on the teacher's desk and the shafts of faint afternoon light coming in from the upper casement windows.

We were a small group, our numbers at the American Community School greatly reduced by both the civil war and the war with Israel. As tensions in the city escalated, most diplomats packed up their families and returned to their own countries. The only new influx of expats to the city were 1,500 US Marines sent by President Reagan to man the five U.S. warships anchored a few kilometres offshore.

After Advanced French, I joined my class on the first floor for Grade Seven English. Mr. Turner examined us with his one good eye while his glass eye stared straight ahead. Its fixed look unnerved me. It was like staring at a camera. I imagined it photographing my secret thoughts—a bionic eye with special powers.

"A bomb has exploded nearby, at the American Embassy," Mr. Turner informed the class once we had taken our seats. "Fortunately for us, our school remains unscathed." He paused, but only for a breath. "Please take out your copies of Twain's *The Prince and the Pauper*. We will read aloud, beginning at Chapter Three."

My hands picked up the paperback novel and flipped mechanically to the correct page while my mind wrestled to process this new information. I raised my hand. "How close did we come to being hit?"

Mr. Turner's glass eye stared at a distant spot behind my head while his good eye looked out the window. "We'll find out soon enough," he said.

It was a relief to get lost in the story of a faraway place and forget about what was going on in the city around us.

"Be careful on the way home," Mr. Turner said before dismissing the class for the day. "See you tomorrow."

Our regular route through the campus was blocked off by red tape marked DANGER. We were shepherded into two lines and made to show our identity cards and hand our schoolbags over for inspection by armed French military police at three different makeshift checkpoints inside the gate, before finally being given permission to exit onto the street. Sirens blared nearby, and traffic on the main street was barred. The empty street was an eerie sight compared to the usual noisy tangle of cars and pedestrians.

My brother walked a few paces ahead of me. "Did you hear it?" I asked him. I watched the back of his head nod yes.

"I was in art," he mumbled.

It was hard to hear from behind. I got as close to him as I could, but the passage was only wide enough to walk single file.

"We left class and went there." He stepped onto the street to avoid a pile of garbage on the sidewalk. In the absence of waste removal services, the citizens of Beirut piled their garbage in huge stinking mounds on the sidewalk. Those nearest to the beach threw it into the Mediterranean. After over twelve years of anarchy and civil war, the city resembled a massive garbage dump.

"What do you mean? Where did you go?" Our school never went on field trips of any kind; it was too dangerous to leave the gated compound.

"Mrs. Gunthrey wanted to see what had happened. Her husband works at the embassy and she needed to make sure he was all right. So she took us there."

"Was he okay?" I kicked at an empty sardine can, shuffling it back and forth between my feet like a soccer ball.

"Took a while, but we found him. He was all white. Covered in dust. He thought his arm might be broken. He was holding onto a woman whose face was cut up. Her eyes were full of blood."

After that, my brother was quiet for a long time. I kept my head down and followed his footsteps exactly, walking in the street to sidestep more garbage and a car parked on the sidewalk, also a common occurrence in this city without traffic lights or police surveillance.

"I saw a car wrapped around a telephone pole," my brother said in a voice so low I thought maybe I hadn't heard him properly.

"What? How?"

"It's the force of the blast," he said. "It picks up anything in its way."

When we got home, Maman was frantic. She called to us from the balcony. "*Enfin!*" she said, raising her hands into the air. In her white dress she reminded me of our old Catholic priest in his vestments, raising his arms to say the blessing over the communion bread and wine. "You're safe!" She disappeared through the open kitchen door, the heavy drapes shutting her from sight. Moments later, she was on the street trying to hug us both at the same time. "*Oh, mon Dieu,*" she said. "*Oh, mon Dieu.*" She caressed my braid, running her hands up and down its length.

She leaned her shoulder into our front door as she turned the key in the lock. "*Aidez-moi,*" she said. It was a bullet-proof door, couched in leather, and extremely heavy.

"A few more minutes, and I was coming after you." Her hands fluttered up to her face, then to her dishevelled hair.

It occurred to me that maybe she'd been afraid to leave the apartment to come looking for us. Maybe that was why she never met us after school or walked us there or back. I had no idea what she did all day while we were at school and my father was working. I'd never thought about it before. She was always waiting for us when we arrived, cooking something up for our dinner, eager for news of how the day had gone.

"Come, sit, I made you some *chocolat chaud,*" she said. "Tell me what happened."

I had nothing to say, beyond my experience in the library. My brother drank his cocoa in a few quick drafts. His face was tight and strained as if he hadn't slept in a long time. He didn't tell our mother what he'd told me, just went to his room and shut the door.

"The radio says there are many dead," my mother said. She burst into tears, then jumped up from the couch. "I need to contact your father. I need to tell him you're home. Safe." She grabbed the telephone on its stand in the hallway, held it to her ear, then slammed it back down. "No connection."

She continued trying, then slid down onto the sofa and remained there, crumpled up. She tried to smooth her skirt over her knees but then slumped her shoulders over, as if exhausted by the effort.

"I heard the blast from over here. I knew it was something big. There was footage on BBC TV... I saw people lying in the street outside your compound. I have no way to reach your father at *le quartier générale*. I tried calling the school, but *le telephone était mort, comme d'habitude.*" She started to cry again. She stared at the television screen, where a reporter with a British accent stood in front of a demolished building.

When my father finally came home around seven that night she was wild. "*On sort d'ici!*" she said, her voice a hysterical shriek. She was still wearing the white summery dress, but it was wrinkled and limp, like a paper napkin. Her hair had come loose on one side, while the other was still pinned up, giving her an unbalanced look. Pin in hand, she tried to coax her thick hair into its twist, but it kept falling back around her face.

My father sat down on the sofa and fiddled with the transistor radio on the coffee table. "We'll go to Greece for a couple of weeks," he said, "until the city calms down. We'll visit Athens, like you've always wanted—see the Acropolis. From there, we can go to one of the islands. Whichever one you want: Mykonos, Rhodes, Crete. You decide. It's time we took a holiday."

It was enough to quiet my mother. She stopped pacing and came to sit near him.

"But we can't leave for another week." He adjusted the radio dial.

My mother left the couch and stormed into the kitchen. "*Tout de suite!*" she shouted. "*J'en peux plus!*"

"I have work to do in the city. Especially after what's just happened. It took us all by surprise. Even our contacts in the CIA. At least one of them is dead now, maybe two. We've lost our best American sources.

"I'm commanding officer," he continued. "You can't expect me to leave after this disaster. It will take us a week to sort it all out. After that, we can go. We don't even know who's to blame."

"You are to blame," my mother shouted, her angry face framed by the kitchen doorway.

Still holding the buzzing radio, my father walked to their bedroom and shut the door.

NEXT MORNING, HE wouldn't let us go to school. "It will be a zoo down there," he said. "They're still searching for bodies."

BBC News set the death toll at 63. Over half were Lebanese embassy employees; 17 were Americans. The rest, unnamed, were bystanders. An additional 120 or so were wounded.

"How could a car bomb kill so many people?" I asked.

"It was a delivery van packed with 2,000 pounds of explosives parked at the very front of the building," my brother said. "A suicide bomber."

That night, my brother's screams pierced the apartment. I woke from a deep sleep to the hellish sound of his cries. The hallway light was on, and my parents' bedroom door was open.

My father stood in the hallway, holding his burgundy bathrobe closed with his hand. One end of the terry cloth belt hung loosely from his side. The rest of the belt trailed behind him. "*Fais quelque chose*," he said to my mother. "Do something."

I could hear the sound of her sobbing mixed with my brother's. I wondered what else my brother had seen that day that he hadn't told me about.

My father went to the storage closet in the brightly lit hallway and pulled out a pale yellow suitcase with one hand while he held his bathrobe with the other. After a few minutes, four suitcases lined the hall. He turned to look at me.

I was sitting up in bed, chin resting on my knees. Should I tell him what my brother had told me? "Yesterday," I began.

"Find your bathing suit," my father said. "We're going to Greece."

"Skipping school?" I asked. "For how long?" But he had followed my mother into my brother's darkened room.

"THERE WILL BE other dances," my mother said the next morning. She was cooking eggs at the stove.

"Yes," I said, "but this is a Sadie Hawkins dance. The girls ask the boys." I hoped to appeal to her sense of women's rights.

"It must be an American thing," my mother said dismissively.

She lifted her flipper and brought it down—*smack!*— against the counter, then whacked it again hard, then harder still.

"*Maman, qu'est-ce que tu fais?*" I asked. She brought the spatula down one more time and the thing split apart, the metal front and screws clattering to the floor. With the wooden handle left in her hand, she pointed at the spot where she'd been hammering. I picked up a crushed cockroach the size of my index finger, its grotesque body completely flattened by my mother's manic energy. I threw it over the balcony railing.

It was a final affront. When she put my father's plate in front of him at the table, her hands were shaking. "It could have been one of us out there, walking by the embassy," she said. She was still standing by the table in her bathrobe. My father's eggs were getting cold.

I wasn't sure what to do. Should I start eating? Sitting down at the table together to eat was a non-negotiable aspect of our family. My father, who liked to eat his food hot, was always served last. Once he had his plate, the rest of us would begin to eat. I picked up my fork. I was hungry, but I was also scared of my mother. I had never seen her this angry.

"Our children could have been killed while sitting at their school desks. We can't go on like this."

My father held the pepper shaker over his eggs. "Please sit down."

But my mother refused. "They don't want us here, organizing their city for them, working for peace." She spat out her last word like it was something rancid.

My father started eating.

"The Greek resorts are all closed in April," my mother said. "It's too cold to swim in the Mediterranean."

"We'll rent a jeep in Crete," my father said, "and drive up into the mountains. The orchards will be full of fruit." He took a sip of his coffee. "I know people who can get us through the airport."

"What are you saying?" my mother asked. Her hands gripped the back of the chair.

"There's a possibility it may soon be under siege. It's a good time to take a little holiday." My father lifted the *Egyptian Daily News* so that his face was hidden behind the front page.

"I'm running a bath," my mother said. She got up from

the table and headed for the bathroom. I rifled through the pile of newspapers beside my father, looking for the comics section.

When she emerged a half hour later her hair was pinned up and she wore a fresh dress. It was a relief to see her put back together. In her hand were drawings pulled from a sketchbook. "I went into Stephen's room, to check on him and gather up his laundry," she said woodenly. "I found these on his desk." She held them out to my father, who was still seated next to me at the dining room table, surrounded by dirty dishes and headlines. She didn't realize my brother had followed her out of his room and was standing behind her.

"Hey," he said, reaching for his drawings, "those are mine." He looked like he'd slept in his jeans, and his eyes were sunken into his head.

He grabbed the papers, but my father refused to let go. I leaned over his arm to see. There was an eyeball that was also a picture of the Earth, with its continents and oceans drawn in coloured pencil behind the pupil and iris. To the side of the globe a large wound gaped open, with blood spurting out and dripping off the page.

My father lifted the corner of the page to see what was underneath.

There my brother had drawn people lying on their backs, their faces distorted into screaming holes. Under them were other bodies, mangled and twisted into strange positions. Blood everywhere. Over the nightmarish scene hovered a huge pair of disembodied eyes, partly obscured by cumulus clouds.

"You had no right to come into my room like that," my brother said.

My father placed the drawings face down on the table

beside the *Jerusalem Post*.

"At the back of the fridge," he said, "in a cookie tin, are 10,000 US dollars. If ever the fighting gets so bad that we need to leave in a hurry, and the airport is closed, we'll use the money to hire a rowboat to take us across the Mediterranean. I want you both to know that," he said, looking me full in the face. "Just in case."

Getting It Wrong

Eve Corbel

One afternoon when I went to the daycare to pick up my three-year-old granddaughter, I discovered that she had been telling the kids and staff that "My grandma threw my mummy in the bushes." In fact, one day in 1979 I had been walking with her mother, then age six, on the sidewalk along a thoroughfare used by trucks, when I had a premonition that a truck would crash right beside us. I grabbed her up and ran away from the road into a grassy area lined with shrubbery, and we fell together into a clump of beaked hazel. A moment later a semi trailer went over on its side and screamed down the road for a good fifty yards, throwing off sparks and debris all the way. No one was hurt, including us, and the incident entered family legend. At a recent Sunday dinner, someone had brought it up and "My grandma threw my mummy in the bushes" is what the three-year-old went away with.

As I explained the story to the daycare workers, I wondered how much my own version might have changed in the thirty-five years since the incident. At this point I had read about half of *Being Wrong: Adventures in the Margin of Error* by Kathryn Schulz, a wonderful meditation on getting stuff wrong as a cornerstone of human intelligence, imagination and creativity. She starts with the errors of our senses, such as the superior mirage (a trick of arctic light), the inferior mirage (the shimmering pool of water we "see" on the sun-baked highway ahead) and inattentional blindness, referring to the fact that we see with our brain, not with our eyes. When we know we are being tricked, we enjoy it—in apprehending art, jokes, optical illusions and magic tricks, for example—but otherwise we don't.

Then she considers other errors, mainly our propensity to respond intuitively and instantly to what's going on around us and, based on this hastily gathered evidence, to jump to conclusions that are often mistaken. To compound matters, we cling to these errors with astonishing tenacity. There is even a word for an erroneous but unshakable belief: *mumpsimus*, said to have been coined inadvertently by a medieval monk known for reciting the phrase "quod in ore mumpsimus" instead of the proper "quod in ore sumpsimus" ("which we have taken into the mouth"). *Sumpsimus* means "we have taken" in English; *mumpsimus* translates as nonsense in any language. When someone finally challenged the monk, he snapped back that he had been saying it that way for forty years and would not throw out "my old *mumpsimus* for your new *sumpsimus*." In 1545, Henry VIII referred to both words in a speech, giving *mumpsimus* royal approval.

It seems to us that we remember things as though they happened yesterday, but we get the details wrong, more and more of them over time, in such a systematic way that the attrition, as Schulz puts it, "can be plotted on a graph, in what is known, evocatively, as the 'Ebbinghaus curve of forgetting.'" That is consistent with what scientists believe now, that a memory is not stashed holus-bolus in the brain but is reassembled by various bodily bits and functions when we send for it.

GIVEN WHAT ELSE we know about the nature of memory, perhaps the breadth of the human margin of error shouldn't surprise us. In researching plagiarism as part of my teaching on editorial ethics, I came across "Speak, Memory," an article by Oliver Sacks about his own distortions of memory. The experience, for instance, of describing a vivid memory only to have a sibling declare that it didn't happen, or happened to someone else; or of confidently composing an essay and later being taken aback to discover that one has already written that essay—much of it verbatim, in an act of innocent self-plagiarism. Should we be reassured by the fact that even a top-notch neurologist is susceptible to these errors, or should we be alarmed? Brain imaging, he says, shows that a vivid memory brings on "widespread activation in the brain" in a pattern that is the same whether the memory is real or false. He mentions the work of Elizabeth Loftus, who has implanted fake memories in people's brains with "disquieting success." In a *ScienceDaily* post that I read on the bus two days later ("Your memory is no video camera"), a neuroscientist named Donna Jo Bridge says that the human memory "is built to change, not regurgitate facts." To cope with the continuous fast changes around us, our memory constantly rearranges bits, supplanting the old with the new, and creating "a story to fit [our] current world." Thanks to MRI technology, we can pinpoint the exact moment when new information pops in and colonizes an older memory. What the—? No wonder we get stuff wrong!

And the human memory is suggestible in even more ways. Politicians have more extramarital affairs than other people, right? No, but they get more publicity, so the information is more available, so that's what we think. If we see the words *bananas* and *vomit* together, we hook them up as cause and effect. If we have heard the word *eat* recently, we are more likely to complete "SO_P" as *soup* than *soap*. And if you want us to vote for higher school funding, put the polling station in a school. Bold type, high contrast, rhyming slogans, prominent blue or red in the copy—these, not careful research and thought, are the elements of messages that we find most convincing.

These last humiliating tidbits come from another wonderful book, *Thinking, Fast and Slow*, a remaindered copy of which literally fell into my hands from the sale shelf in a crowded bookstore. The author, the economist and psychologist Daniel Kahneman, offers another sort of entrance to questions about why we get things wrong, and why we won't let go of erroneous beliefs. It has to do with the human cognitive process, he says, and its two main informants: System 1, which is intuitive, emotional and lightning-fast in interpreting input; and System 2, the cooler head, which works slowly to compare things, weigh the options, follow the rules. System 2 also keeps us civil when we feel the urge to act on an extreme feeling. Both systems live everywhere, not lodged in the left or right brain, and there's some overlap. But generally, System 1 has its antennae out all the time, picking up data like a Twitter addict; then it trolls through the memory, stashing bits wherever they will strengthen associations already in place, and discarding the bits that don't. System 2 is the careful, analytical, sober second thought, but with limited resources, like a fact checker with no access to a library or the internet. Both of these systems are good and magical and necessary, Kahneman writes, and both are a bit lazy. They put together the best story from what comes to hand, in a process he calls WYSIATI: What You See Is All There Is. System 1 infers much from little and reduces unfamiliar material to heuristics and bias. For example, the question "How much would you contribute to save an endangered species?" is easily replaced in our minds by the simpler question "How much emotion do I feel when I think of dying dolphins?" and we don't even notice it. System 2, which doesn't get out much and usually fails to notice when System 1 is introducing error by elision, "casually endorses" a lot of erroneous associations. In other words, our minds manage the data load by maintaining associative order: "everything reinforcing everything else." One can't help thinking of the guy who searches for his lost keys under a streetlamp, rather than where he thinks he lost them, because the light is better there. We suppress ambiguity, and therefore we see a world that is probably more coherent and user-friendly than if we tried to absorb and process all the random sensory input available. That is a healthy impulse, but it requires intellectual shortcuts.

And some stubbornness. We feel very sure of our perceptions and beliefs, and we go to some trouble to stay that way. We deny, deploy defences, confabulate, refuse or reinterpret evidence—anything to maintain our moorings. "Certainty is lethal to two of our most redeeming and humane qualities, imagination and empathy," Kathryn Schulz writes. Our instincts serve us well. We need them to think, to live, to enjoy living.

AT THAT POINT I set down *Being Wrong* for a couple of days, during which I happened to hear a Radiolab podcast called "Are You Sure?" It included the story of Penny Beerntsen, an American woman who was raped by a stranger. Even as the man attacked her, she had the presence of mind to get a good look at him and try to scratch him to leave marks (this was 1985, before DNA testing was considered reliable). Shortly afterward, Beerntsen identified the man from mug shots. She also picked him out of an eight-man police lineup: not only did she recognize him immediately, but the sight of him set her to trembling and raised the hair on the back of her neck. The attacker was convicted and sent to prison. Some years later he persuaded the court to run DNA tests on the evidence, and it turned out that he was not the man who had attacked her.

Talk about being wrong! How could that happen? Beerntsen did everything right. She fought back, then tried to focus on gathering evidence, then listened to her own body at the police lineup. Can anyone be sure of anything, ever?

I plunged into *Being Wrong*, Part III, The Experience of Error, about our epic struggle to prove to ourselves that we are not wrong. Sometimes we do change our beliefs, but even then, as Daniel Kahneman reports, we tend to move seamlessly, or blindly, through the points between "thinking that we are right and knowing that we were wrong," either too quickly or too gradually to notice the shift. And thanks to the endless updates to our memory—also not noticed by us—we remember our former beliefs as being much closer to our current ones than they actually were, expunging the memory of having changed our minds. When we do fall into the "terrain of pure wrongness," as Penny Beerntsen did, or anyone who loses a wad in a market downturn, or gets betrayed by a lover, we're lost.

Our ability to incorporate error can also be affected by our mood at the moment, our place of residence, our time of life. Teenagers are adored and loathed for being obdurate, for example, and the wisdom of our elders owes a lot to their growing certainty that one cannot be sure of anything. (What we know now about the act of remembering—to gather wisps and to wait for the processes to line up—is exactly how it feels, physically, to me and my sixty-something friends.) Things move more quickly and effortlessly for younger folks, so it is no wonder they are more taken aback when they find out they erred, and no wonder they are more given to reconstructions: the time-frame defence (my timing was off), the near-miss defence (I was almost right), the out-of-left-field defence (I got messed up by the unforeseeable) and so on.

When I turned the page to chapter 11, Denial and Acceptance, what should I find but the story of Penny Beerntsen, the woman who misidentified her attacker. Schulz points out that although eyewitness accounts are the most convincing evidence in courtrooms, they are appallingly faulty: the most careful and observant witnesses get about 25 percent of the details wrong. (The rest of them get 26 to 80 percent wrong.) Yet we cling to our memories and beliefs, most of which are formed from crude, tiny data, and we tend to deny evidence to the contrary, or bend it to fit.

Reading this I was reminded of a workshop for magazine publishers a few months earlier, led by Craig Silverman, a journalist with a special interest in media errors, corrections, accuracy and verification—very useful in these days of fabricated stories, doctored images, robot social media feeds and general dreck. Among other things, he spoke of our reluctance to let go of wrong information once we have accepted it as truth. He mentioned a study subtitled "The Persistence of Political Misperceptions," which showed that after people read and accepted false and unsubstantiated data—about the Iraqi weapons of mass destruction, for example—and then were given corrected information, few of them changed their minds. For a good number of subjects there was even a backfire effect: the factual, substantiated information only strengthened their original (erroneous) conviction.

Our refusal to live in doubt is largely a healthy instinct, Schulz writes—invoking Plato, Augustine, Freud, Kübler-Ross and others—when it is "sincere and subconscious." It protects us from the anxiety and horror of feeling wrong all the time, or (shudder) constantly second-guessing and dithering, and living among others who do the same. But the price we pay is high. What about Holocaust denial, to bring up a painful example? Or climate change resistance? Or the "death panels" freakout of 2009, when Sarah Palin raised the spectre of bureaucrat-driven euthanasia when the US government broached the subject of socialized medicine?

The day after I read the Penny Beerntsen chapter in *Being Wrong*, I tuned in to another Radiolab podcast, "The Man Behind the Maneuver," put together by a journalist who as a child had been saved from choking to death by a school nurse who applied the Heimlich Maneuver. This journalist found Henry Heimlich (now in his nineties) living in Cincinnati and went to talk to him. It is surprising and wonderful to hear the story of the Maneuver from Heimlich himself, whose work is so legendary that I was amazed to hear he was still alive. And there's more. Not long after his rise to fame and celebrity (such as appearances on TV to teach Johnny Carson and David Letterman how to do the Maneuver), Heimlich declared that the use of the Maneuver would relieve asthma, and later he proposed it as a treatment for drowning victims. On a roll, he then offered cures for cancer and AIDS that were, to spin it as kindly as possible, eccentric. Heimlich's colleagues and his own family finally managed to get these claims discredited, but it took years because of Heimlich's absolute certainty, backed up by his authority, reinforced by his show-biz fame. In 2005, the Red Cross declared that back-slapping—still our instinct when someone is choking—is just as effective as the

Heimlich Maneuver. Five back thumps between the shoulder blades, to be exact, then the "abdominal thrusts," as the Maneuver is now officially known. In the Radiolab interview with Heimlich years later, though, he still sounds certain.

We all strive to be certain. Certainty is a good feeling, even a necessary one if your well-being depends on it— if you're an elected official, say, or a witness to a crime, or a mother of teenagers. That's because not only do we feel more confident when we are certain, but also we are easily seduced by apparent certainty and confidence in others. Studies have shown that we much prefer the decisive, assured political candidate (or teacher, or boss) to the less certain one, regardless of other qualities: statistically we are more likely to vote for the confident liar than the good guy who voices doubts. At a teacher training workshop I once attended, the instructors were unequivocal on what to do if one had so much as the shadow of a doubt in the classroom: "*Act as if.*" We also prefer doctors who are certain—even if they turn out to be mistaken, even if we have read the UK study that found clinicians to be "completely wrong" about diagnoses 40 percent of the time.

We invest the confident one with even more credibility and authority if she is taller, has a certain kind of face and, especially, if she is a celebrity. Heimlich's fame as a lifesaver and TV personality was rock solid when he recommended the Maneuver for people who were drowning; otherwise he would have been ridden out of town on a rail. And one dynamic, attractive, confident celebrity like Jenny McCarthy, the actor and TV host who argues a causal connection between childhood vaccines and autism, can convince a lot more people a lot more quickly than a thousand practitioners of the plodding, painstaking, incremental work of medical science.

BY THE TIME I was about three-quarters of the way through *Being Wrong*, I was half-convinced that Grandma had probably never fallen into any bushes with Mummy, or thrown her in, or anything else. Meanwhile, bits of apparently related material had begun to come in from all directions and all media, à la *Night of the Living Dead*. Articles on paper and online, blog posts, novels, radio podcasts, ten-year-old books in the endcaps at the library, conversations overheard on the train, meaningless TV shows suggested by my partner's Netflix account—everything interrogated or answered everything else. Was this a magical instance of interdependent co-arising? Or had I become a walking example of the tendency to strive for "cognitive ease," as Daniel Kahneman calls it, cherry-picking incoming data so that everything reinforces everything else?

Only a few days after tucking into the Kahneman, I pulled my *New Yorker* out of the mailbox and found "The Gift of Doubt," a piece about the late Albert O. Hirschman, an economist. It starts with the story of a nineteenth-century railway megaproject in the northeastern United States: a tale of extensive planning, testing and predicting, and of colossal underestimating of time, trouble and expense. Hirschman was also a planner of megaprojects, and he was particularly interested in "unintended consequences and perverse outcomes," having observed that when everything goes wrong with a large project, people find solutions that they had never dreamed of, solutions much more elegant and useful and long-lasting than the original objectives, forged from the heat of terrific unexpected stress. He wondered if "the only way in which we can bring our creative resources fully into play is by misjudging the nature of the task"—to plan it and undertake it as if it were "routine, simple, undemanding of genuine creativity."

Well, I have never had responsibility for an infrastructure project, but I can name a number of stories and articles and books and magazines that would never have been written, designed, produced or marketed, had their authors and publishers known what they were getting into. My heart goes out to the proprietors of the 35 percent of small businesses that don't make it to the five-year mark because of optimism bias, but isn't it better, existentially, to have loved and lost?

And speaking of failing, I've seen more published eurekas, op-eds and how-to's about failure in the last six months than in my whole life before that. Failing is good. Failing is natural. It's all right to fail. Embrace failure. Make your children embrace failure. Failing makes you smart. *Adapt: Why Success Always Starts with Failure. The Rise: Creativity, the Gift of Failure, and the Search for Mastery. Brilliant Blunders: From Darwin to Einstein—Colossal Mistakes by Great Scientists That Changed Our Understanding of Life and the Universe. You Are Not So Smart* (subtitle ends with "and 46 Other Ways You're Deluding Yourself").

Some of this writing—maybe all of it—is illuminating and bracing: for example, Paul Tough's book *How Children Succeed,* showing that success is born of curiosity, perseverance and resourcefulness, rather than high test scores; and *To Forgive Design: Understanding Failure*, by Henry Petroski, who has been writing for thirty years about buildings that fall down, bridges that collapse, dams that break and other failures that alert us to "weaknesses in reasoning, knowledge, and performance that all the successful designs may not even hint at."

But wait. Error and failure are different, aren't they? If a bridge gives way fifty years after it was designed and constructed, having supported many more vehicles weighing many more tons than the engineers could have predicted, is that a design error? Well, sometimes it is. In at least one case, in Quebec, an investigation showed that some small components of a failed bridge, called eyebars, could wear down but could not be inspected.

In fact, there is so much failure writing that a body of pushback lit is also accumulating. In an online post, Sam McNerney pinpoints the typical agenda: that it is admirable (and fashionable) to fail, but only if we eventually achieve success, which is measured in terms of fame and/or fortune. No one writes a story about their permanent failure, and no one wants to read such a story. Liza Mundy, in her article "Losing Is the New Winning," mentions eight new books on the subject. She notes that the failure fad opens the door for the Eliot Spitzers of the world to exhibit their pain, absolve themselves, be admired and then get back in the race. It's important to forgive people for doing bad things, but as Mundy writes, "When is a public figure's failure a sign of abiding character flaws, and when is it a harbinger of growth?" The same can be said of civilians.

There are interesting connections to be explored between cognitive error and failure, and the McNerney and Mundy articles and others like them raise good points. But both *Being Wrong* and *Thinking, Fast and Slow* are mentioned, and I can't help thinking that in landing the evidence, the authors got some bycatch. Both Kathryn Schulz and Daniel Kahneman are clear on why they went to the trouble of writing it all down for us. Both writers are enchanted by the elegant, sophisticated workings of our minds, and both speak of public conversation rather than private redemption.

Kahneman, who describes human intuition as "marvelous," says that his purpose is to give readers the skills to "identify and understand errors of judgment and choice," in ourselves and others, "by providing a richer and more precise language to discuss them." Schulz ends her book with accounts of people and institutions who have acknowledged error, apologized for it, gathered data on what went wrong, and changed policies and practices to fix it. Her examples include Beth Israel Deaconess Medical Center and the US commercial aviation industry, whose errors can be devastating. The emphasis is on striving for consistent quality, measuring and analyzing results, making decisions based on real data rather than assumptions and guesswork, apologizing for error and changing whatever caused that error. Being right brings out the worst in us, Schulz says, but when we do accommodate fallibility and acknowledge wrongness, we become more compassionate. For starters, we can learn to listen—even in the noisy, egocentric, brand-crazy society that swirls around us.

Listening is also the example offered by Albert O. Hirschman, the megaproject planner who was interested in unexpected endings, and who avoided conventional criteria for measuring success. In surveying large World Bank-sponsored projects on four continents, ranging from irrigation to power transmission, he recommended that a project not be evaluated just by measuring benefits, but also by asking how many "conflicts...it brought in its wake," and "crises... it occasioned and passed through." He welcomed adversity, and he welcomed doubt. Kathryn Schulz, too, says that we could do worse than to remember Socrates, who tried to fill his students with uncertainty—not fearfulness but *aporia*, "active, investigative doubt."

At this point, part of me wants to go back into my journals and read my immediate account of the day in 1979 when I picked up my daughter and ran until we fell into the bushes. Having read about human error over the last year, I'm pretty sure I know what I will find, or not find, in the journals. Another part of me wants to leave it alone and wait to see how the story continues to evolve—by elision, or embellishment, or just plain error.

Expos Nation

ADAM GOPNIK

I ATTENDED THE very first home opener of the Montreal Expos, and for the next decade I never missed another. From 1969 to 1981, when I left my hometown for New York, I saw them all—a better attendance record, albeit more easily accomplished, than I had managed at any of my other schools. For the first eight years, the home openers, always in a wintry Montreal April, were played outdoors in Jarry Park: small banks of weary snow, crusted with black grime, ran right around the warning track in the outfield. Later, the games took place in the endlessly maligned Olympic Stadium, where the snow floated in through the vast hole above centre field; eventually, the "retractable" roof got stuck in place, hovering sadly in the air.

To say that I loved the Expos hardly describes it. The first piece of mine to be published in *The New Yorker*, the great event of my professional life, was about them—about the (invented) difficulties of being an art historian, as I was pretending to become then, and an Expos fan. In fact, I shut my eyes, and I think, God help me, that I can actually summon that opening-day lineup from forty-five years past. Let me try (no googling or post hoc emendation, I promise): first base, Bob Bailey; second base, Gary Sutherland; shortstop, Bobby Wine; third base, Coco Laboy; right field,

Rusty Staub; centre field, someone like Don Hahn; left field, Mack Jones; catcher, John Bateman; pitcher, Mudcat Grant. How did I do? Let me see...not too badly, though it is strange I forgot it was Maury Wills—the only original Expo who had any kind of shot at the Hall of Fame—who actually started at shortstop. Strange and perhaps significant: I edit out their small chance at excellence, because we didn't really ask that the Expos be excellent. They were merely special, in ways that I suspect the far more successful teams—I almost wrote "franchises"—were not.

When they died in 2004, ten years ago this October, and found a new life as the Washington Nationals, the part of me that took its identity from baseball died too, and left me with little love for the game. (I have never been out to the new Citi Field in New York, and only once to the new Yankee Stadium.) Not long ago, I learned that there was a movement—an actual, credible-sounding push, fronted by one-time Expos first baseman Warren Cromartie—to bring the team back to Montreal, just as the Jets came back to Winnipeg. It got me thinking about the Expos, and what they meant to me, and to Montreal. I realized that my love for the city I still think of as my hometown, and some other, more complicated things about my adolescence and my relationship with my father and family, were, weirdly enough, tied up in my feelings about this lost ball club. I went out and talked to people who knew truths about the Expos that I did not.

WHAT MADE THE Expos special? First, and most important, it was their look, their logo. Jerry Seinfeld said, memorably and accurately, that when we root for pro sports teams we're really rooting for clothes, since the players have no real connection to the teams, and they change allegiances at the flick of an additional zero. But to say that we are rooting for laundry is to say, in another sense, that we are rooting for flags. Team colours—the Dodgers blue, the Yankees pinstripe, even the Maple Leafs maple leaf—are the heraldry of the cities in which they play. Since cities are the largest unit for which we can credibly claim the emotions—love, attachment, patriotism—that nationalists annex to nations, the laundry our hired athletes wear assumes an outsize symbolic importance. The uniforms of teams become the flags of towns.

All of this to say, simply, that the Expos had a *great* flag. Their tricoloured uniform and cap—red, white, and blue in neat pin-wheeling form—remain hugely popular to this day, long after their demise. A circus cap, a bowling team logo—everything that was said against it was part of what gave it charm. It was the rare heraldic symbol that refused to take itself entirely seriously. And yet, truth be told, from a pure design perspective it wasn't all that hot. It was a kind of triple pun: a stylized evocation of a ball and glove, which also spells out M-B-E, perhaps indicating "Montreal," "Baseball," and "Expos," but also seeming to suggest C-B, the initials of Charles Bronfman, the majority owner and Seagram heir. Still, the logo didn't have to be articulate to be affecting. Whatever it meant, it meant Montreal.

The team's colours were the same as those of the Canadiens: Montreal, like Luke Skywalker's Tatooine, was a planet with two suns, and the Habs were always much the brighter. But where the Canadiens' colours evoked turn-of-the-century amateur athletic clubs, on the Expos they had a pleasingly elementary look, like a kindergarten's collective ideal of a baseball cap. The Expos always acted as the happy-go-lucky younger brother to the Habs' grim older one, burdened as the Canadiens were with the eldest sibling's duty to win, and win again. The Habs were serious; the Expos were not.

In those days, the Habs were more of a church than a club. Tickets to the Forum were as hard won as tickets to an audience with the Pope, and the atmosphere inside the arena was quiet, brutal, and expectant. I still recall, having somehow found a ticket for a game in 1971, jumping up and down when Claude Larose—Claude Larose!—scored; a man one row back asked me, in French, never to do so again. No one had trouble finding a seat for the Expos, and no one minded when you jumped up and down, even if it was for no reason at all.

And then there was a certain magic to the choice of the name, which was part of the legacy of Expo 67 itself, and redolent with the charm of a certain moment in Montreal history. The hangover of Expo 67 was more than merely positive—Expo was the last great world's fair, the finale in a great sequence that began in the mid-nineteenth century and briefly turned mercantile cities into celebratory ones. Even in the mid-'70s, the nationalist pop band Beau Dommage could still sing of Expo positively: "*En soixante-sept tout était beau / c'était l'année d'l'amour, c'était l'année d'l'Expo / chacun son beau passeport avec une belle photo*" ("In sixty-seven everything was aglow / it was the year of love, it was the year of Expo / everyone had a beautiful passport with a beautiful photo"). Everything at Expo worked, and everything was wonderful. The Expos name carried that triumph onto the ball field.

At the time, the city was officially in crisis. The October Crisis itself, of course, took place a year after that opening game, and there was always the slow, creeping sense that the anglophone side of the city was collapsing. Head offices closed; friends fled to Toronto; the English-language

Montreal Star would shut down a few years later. Of course, no teenager can ever cheat his own teenage years of a sense of excitement. With that truth told, however, Montreal in those years really was a unique mix of small town and big city. Neatly divided by boulevard Saint-Laurent, the two solitudes nonetheless leaked into each other as much as they rubbed against each other: my younger brothers and sisters, for instance, all went to a French-speaking school. (By a predictable irony, this meant I was the only one who later became a passionate francophile.)

Yet the American cliché of the city as "French" in some MGM-backlot way was wildly misleading: It was no more like Paris than it was like Baltimore. Its special quality was not polished elegance but off-centre eccentricity, and this at a time when most of the great cities of North America were in a decline from which there seemed to be no escape. My own birthplace of Philadelphia had turned desolate; the New York to which I already imagined immigrating was—in movies, at least—a bitter, resistant landscape of steaming manholes and shuttered shops and pornography grind houses.

In that company, Montreal seemed dreamlike even to those who were awake in it. There was a thriving downtown. To shop mooningly in the Ogilvy department store, still Scottish in feeling, with its Christmas windows unchanged in a quarter century, was to feel in touch with the old Empire. To have lunch—which my expensive, old-fashioned girlfriend (now my expensive, old-fashioned wife) loved to do—at Eaton's, with its ninth-floor recreation of the dining room of the SS *Île de France*, was to inhabit the kind of happy, bourgeois civilization that had already been atomized in "safe" cities elsewhere. You could also spend a night on rue Saint-Denis, which, though not Parisian, was French, or go to any of the thriving Hungarian cafés, and feel something more than a touristic taste of an older, Middle European culture. A summer night at La Ronde, or a winter morning skiing on Mount Royal—there was a gentleness to Montreal then, which was, I suppose, largely inseparable from its provincialism. (This was true provincialism, that born of a language group enclosed from a larger world; the Québécois provincialism was extended, as much by indifference as benevolence, to the smaller provincialisms, Jewish and Hungarian and Haitian, that it superintended.)

Montreal was what I can only call a naive city. It had a naïveté of tone, an earnestness of spirit, that I still recognize in things from there—Cirque du Soleil to Hugue Dufour's cooking. What they share is that they have not soured on the simpler kinds of pleasure. It was a sweet place, and even those of us who dreamed of a larger horizon and more varied flavours sensed how sweet it was to live there. The Expos were part of that sweetness.

AGAINST ALL THAT charm, my father and I—when we examined the Expos' roster that first spring, over our usual breakfast of Saint-Viateur sesame bagels, or my mother's hyper-dense, artery-clogging croissants—had to balance one huge deficit: they were to be managed by Gene Mauch.

Mauch played an outsize role in our family's baseball heritage and among our family hexes. My father, born and raised in Philadelphia in the '40s and '50s, was a baseball fan of a kind that is now fading from existence. For him, a blue-collar kid who became an Ivy League intellectual, baseball was not one game among many but the only game worth watching. Oh, he liked basketball, of the slow, patterned, set-shot variety. (Today, living on a farm in rural Ontario, he is still indignant at the changes in that sport:

"That's *travelling!*" he says, as some acrobat launches himself from mid-court, dancing three or four steps to the basket.) We enjoyed football together, and he was swept up by the Habs and hockey, though not as entirely or religiously as his son.

Baseball was first among his sports, though, and Gene Mauch had been the sole author of the greatest single disappointment in Phillies history. In September 1964, with the uncharacteristically distinguished Phillies leading the National League by six and a half games with twelve games remaining, Mauch had collapsed under the pressure of a pennant race. He sacrificed his two best pitchers, Jim Bunning and Chris Short, in panicked, short rotation, with predictable results: the Phillies blew the lead, and the pennant, losing ten games in a row. They wouldn't right it until years later when, in one of those ironies that make Greek tragedy such good reading, they did so at the expense of the Expos, to which my entire family had switched its allegiances.

Why sports played a role second only to politics, and equal only to literature, in my large and strange Jewish-scholarly family is a good question, with an answer so obvious it is not really an answer: every family of our kind was like that. Meeting Philip Roth, my father's exact contemporary, many years later in New York, I recognized in him the same predilections: as eager to talk about Bernard Malamud and Henry James as any newly minted freshman, as though college had just started weeks ago and he was trembling on the dangerous brink of declaring himself an English major; his eyes lighting up still brighter when the subject turned to the Yankees and Dodgers of the mid-'40s and '50s. That the entire generation found salvation in English literature and transcendence in North American fandom is strange but consistent.

I wrote once that the genius of a culture resides in those places where people feel safe both joking and not joking, at the same time, about a single subject. My father's generation was like that about baseball. Sufficiently detached not to take it entirely seriously—and sufficiently knowledgeable about the rapacity of capitalism to be skeptical of every owner's motives—they still embraced the pleasure of pro sports. It was a common language they could both share with their lower-middle-class relations (and their own fathers, for that matter) and pass on to their kids. Following sports was a way of obtaining the pleasures of patriotism, of belonging, without the corruptions of chauvinism. For a moment, you could share an emotion with several million other people, without either selling out your values or diminishing your hard-earned distance from your own past.

In any event, Mauch was a throwback—the Little General type. He had a kind of hypnotic fascination with a particular kind of bad baseball player, no longer extant: the pasty, small, scrappy white guy with doggedly acquired skills and no particular athleticism, and he brought a couple with him from Philadelphia to Montreal. Still, his version of small ball, dull though it could be, did not alter the beauty of the ballpark. The Jarry Park stadium, intimate and open to the elements, became and remains a landmark of the park itself. A tiny place that seemed to have been folded as origami rather than built by a construction crew, it seated just over 28,000 fans and felt makeshift and minor league, without enclosed bullpens or a deep-set clubhouse. I was sitting there when man landed on the moon—they did a stick animation on the scoreboard to illustrate it.

Here, however, I have a shameful admission to make: though everyone talked in those days about the wonderful sightlines and immediacy of Jarry Park, and I have spoken of them since, I never quite understood it. It turned out that I suffered, unbeknownst to me, from severe myopia; home plate looked a long way away because everything looked a long way away. That no one spotted this may seem strange, but that was the way it was in my, so to speak, oddly focused family, in which you were expected to have an opinion on Nabokov at the dinner table but had to be walking straight into walls, like a nearsighted silent comedian, before anyone thought to check whether you needed glasses. So: I loved Jarry Park, but its legendary, jewel-box dimensions were mostly lost on me. I watched games, I realize now, mostly by feel. It didn't diminish my enthusiasm. Nothing could.

THE TEAM WASN'T much good back then, but that particularly relaxed and high-spirited Montreal way of celebrating their not-much-goodness drew many people to the park. Fans came, of course, but so did out-of-town journalists. Stunned to discover that the language spoken in Montreal was different from the one spoken in New York, and was said to be French, the reporters would also offer a vastly amusing dictionary of baseball terms—the left fielder, hold your sides, is called the *voltigeur de gauche*! A 1970 *Sports Illustrated* article announced: "'We do not hope our Expos lose the game tonight,' a portly fan explained before a recent game the Expos lost to the Cincinnati Reds, 'but we do not quite expect them to win the game, either. We come out here to have some fun, drink some beer and, of course, to see our Rusty hit the baseball.'"

Then the team got good. Mauch was gone by 1975, eventually replaced by the crusty Dick Williams, and, from around 1978 to 1984, when they stupidly traded their all-star catcher Gary Carter to the Mets, they had as good a team, and as good a chance of winning the World Series, as any in baseball. Not just a good team—potentially a great team, better than any that Canada has seen since, with two no-questions-asked Hall of Famers in Carter and Andre Dawson, and a third, Tim Raines, who should be in the Hall. (His unhappy flirtation with cocaine—he would slide headfirst into second to avoid breaking the vial in his back pocket—and his playing with the under-reported-on Expos hurt his chances of induction.) There was also a fine supporting cast, including the multitalented Cromartie, the fine pitcher Steve Rogers, and the sadly forgotten Ellis Valentine, who was ruined, as Raines luckily was not, by the sport's drug epidemic.

In those years, the supposedly hostile and forbidding Olympic Stadium filled up, averaging more than two million fans each year for around five years—an enormous number back then. Indeed, far from being the mausoleum of legend, Olympic Stadium was a lively, animated place, with fans singing that strange "Valderi, valdera" song and, truly, dancing in the aisles. With my sister Morgan and her husband-to-be, Tom, I went to thirty or forty games each year. (I had written the piece that appeared in *The New Yorker* for them, a few years earlier, as a wedding present.) We even had a family softball team that played up on the McTavish Reservoir against another anglophone family whose names, weirdly, we never knew or demanded, but who showed up reliably, Sunday after Sunday, over some three summers. Montreal was like that, then.

The key, saddening question all Expos fans ask is: Why did they miss? And they *did* miss, never making the World Series and only once playing in the National League Championship Series. There were internal issues—their starting pitching, Rogers aside, was never quite as solid as you might like; the track meet-running game they played, thrilling though it was to watch, was an inefficient way to operate an offence—but mostly they suffered from plain bad luck. That was never more true than on "Blue Monday," the 1981 October playoff game in which, with the National League Championship Series tied at two games each (they played best-of-five in that period) and the Expos at home, Rick Monday, batting for the not-terribly-frightening Los Angeles Dodgers, hit a late home run off Steve Rogers, who had been awkwardly pressed into relief.

Manager Jim Fanning's decision to have Rogers pitch in the ninth instead of going to either of two relievers—Jeff Reardon or Bill Lee—standing in the bullpen bewildered Expos lovers then, and bewilders them now. As Jonah Keri relates in his fine, sad, well-reported history of the team, *Up, Up, and Away*, the ever-direct Lee never had any doubt that he could have done the job: "I tapped my hat, and he brought in Rogers. He gets the first two guys, lefty's coming up, and Fanning leaves him in. Monday ain't gonna hit me. I'm gonna throw him a fastball, then he's gonna foul it off his foot. I'm gonna throw him another fastball, then he's gonna foul it off again. I'm gonna throw him a breaking ball away, he's gonna wave at it, inning over....Fanning, he can't pull the trigger. He has a really nice gun, but he's got no fuckin' bullets in it."

The post-mortem of that inning never ends for Expos fans, but we tend to forget that the series was, after all, tied at two-two, and a Dodger victory was hardly impossible. The truth is the Expos were just unlucky. We edit out pure luck as a cause in sports, and two whole professions, sports writing and statistical analysis, exist to explain exactly why and how things happen as they do. But a whole profession of stock pickers exists, too, and they have been shown time and again to be no more proficient at picking stocks than a chimp throwing darts at the quote pages. We consistently underrate the role of chance, of what just happens, in sports, as we do in life. The Expos, as nearsighted as I was, kept walking into walls.

I WATCHED THE Blue Monday game from a basement apartment in Manhattan, about thirty blocks away from the office building where I met Charles Bronfman, the Expos owner through those years, a few months ago. Even Bronfman cannot remember who exactly came up with the Expos logo: "It was a design firm in Toronto and—I can't recall his name—but he came up with the cap. I showed it to Gene Mauch, and he was shocked. That's not a major league cap! he said. I said, Gene, it may not be a major league cap, but we'll sell a million of these things in the first year. And we did. It's astonishing—the cap is still selling after the team is gone!" Bronfman, now a genial, surprisingly unguarded eighty-three-year-old, lives mostly in New York and Palm Beach, Florida, though he spends "a couple of months in the summer" back in Montreal.

He is frank about what went right, and even more so about what went wrong. "That damn stadium. We were never consulted. We didn't get a word in about it. I said, Don't you think that you should be consulting with your primary tenant, who's going to be *in* the damn place for the next thirty years, as much as you're consulting with the Olympic committee, who'll be in the place for two weeks? But, of course, he"—Jean Drapeau, the mayor of Montreal and the Olympics' hysterical godfather—"insisted that they had to have room for 80,000 people, or whatever it was. Well, it doesn't say they all have to be seated, I said. They could stand on one another's shoulders." Bronfman laughs abruptly. "Okay, that wasn't realistic. But a baseball crowd is 30,000, 32,000—not 80,000. We were going to have a half-empty stadium from the start.

"And once the roof was down—well, Montreal is a cold-weather town, and baseball is a pastoral sport. There's no point in coming out to a ball game unless you can sit out in the summer air. I said to Robert Bourassa, when he was running for premier in 1985, Robert, you're going to win. Why not just put a package of dynamite under the damn thing and be done with it? Generations of Quebecers will thank you for it. But he couldn't."

Bronfman thinks, and most historians agree with him, that the location of the stadium, in Montreal's largely francophone east end, was essential to the peace of the city; a more lucrative spot downtown, near where the Bell Centre is now, was not politically plausible then. "The nice thing in the good years was how much fun it was, how open-hearted the fans were. They were just happy to be watching baseball," he continues. "It was nothing like hockey in Montreal, which was so serious. I remember thinking, actually, when this gets serious it won't be this kind of fun."

I had assumed that, seen from the owner's box, the little vagaries and chances that fill a fan's head would look touchingly unrealistic—that the fan's conviction of the significance of the small triumphs and disasters of the field would seem, to the sports tycoon, naive. I half-expected Bronfman to subvert my own excited Expos mythology, replacing it with a detached businessman's view of the inevitabilities of profit and loss and changing entertainment environments.

So I ask him a little shyly if he actually remembers any of those painful season endings. "Remember them?" he howls. "I recall Blue Monday like it was yesterday." He leans forward. "We had Steve Rogers pitching—a fine pitcher, but he wasn't a reliever. Jeff Reardon couldn't pitch; he was supposedly injured. I can still see the pitch come down and in, and I thought, That's good! Then Monday swung and I thought, Oh, no, it's not.

"Would that one pitch really have changed everything? Oh, absolutely. We would certainly have defeated the Yankees in the World Series—they weren't a strong team that year. I think the Dodgers defeated them in what? Five games?" It was six, actually. "Had we had that championship, everything would have changed. A World Series championship guaranteed attendance for another three to five years, which would have given us a chance to start a new ballpark." He shakes his head. "It just stopped being fun. At the beginning, if you had a bad year, you lost, I don't know, $100,000 or $200,000. Later, it was $10 million. That's no fun at all.

"I remember when it"—the fun—"ended in '91. I said to my business partner—you see, we had a date to go to the ball game. We were getting tiny attendances then. I said, Let's go out to dinner instead of to the ball game, and he said, That's a good idea. So we went—some Italian restaurant on Metcalfe or the like; I remember you had to walk up a long staircase—and we sat down to dinner and I said, You realize what this means, don't you? And he said, I do. And we clinked glasses." He mimes the clink. "And we knew it was over."

WARREN CROMARTIE INSISTS the troubles that plagued the Expos' final years can all be reversed. "What's the difference between now and ten years ago?" he asks, with rehearsed rhetorical energy. "Well, now we have revenue sharing, which we didn't have ten years ago. Now we have Internet marketing. Now we have a wild-card team, which we didn't have ten years ago. Now the US and Canadian dollar are comparable. Now we have television and radio markets in two languages, with dedicated sports networks, which we didn't have ten years ago. Dave Van Horne"—the Expos' longtime play-by-play guy—"had to do the games from his house, because we had no radio contract. Those things are 360 degrees different now," he concludes, with more passion than geometric precision.

Two major league exhibition games were played in Montreal back in March (in the aged Olympic Stadium, of course), and they were widely considered a success. Almost 100,000 fans came to watch the games between the Toronto Blue Jays and the New York Mets, with the Jays filling in, however awkwardly, as the home team. "Baseball Fever Returns!" was the tabloid *Journal de Montréal*'s headline. There were tributes to the late Gary Carter, now enshrined in the Hall of Fame in that tricolour cap, and to a couple of surviving Expos, too. The Montreal Baseball Project, the organization that Cromartie fronts, called the games "a grand slam for Montreal." Though Cromartie is bashful about who exactly the financiers of the "project" are, rumour has it that they include Stephen Bronfman, Charles' son.

The hurdles remain enormous: People like old-fashioned ballparks, but if the new Expos ever did get into the playoffs, it would be too cold to play in Montreal, given the ridiculous late-fall scheduling of the World Series. Movable or part-time domes do exist—they have one in Arizona, where the parallel problem of summer heat governs the city's existence, and there is, of course, that one in Toronto—but it would add yet another expense to the already costly business of building a new stadium downtown. Whoever did it would need deep pockets, and it seems unlikely that the provincial government would dip that far. I fear that if the

Expos did come back—with the old name and the old logo, both of which now belong to Major League Baseball—they would remain a perpetual source of worry. Montreal is once again a thriving place, but not, in truth, a growing one.

There is a secret, though, about the Expos' legacy, one that everyone feels but no one acknowledges. It is this: in many ways, the serious Canadiens have become the happy Expos. As I see with some shock, on my family's annual pilgrimage to the Bell Centre, Habs fans today are more like Expos fans than they are like the Habs fans of the past. The smoking gun pointing to this transformation is the presence of Youppi!, the Expos' fuzzy orange mascot, whom the Habs have adopted; he would have been as unimaginable at the old Montreal Forum as an oompahpah band. For intensity of attachment, the Bell Centre throng remains one of the best sports crowds in the world—only FC Barcelona and the Pittsburgh Steelers, in my limited experience, command the same degree of attention and regard from their cities—but it has little in common with the old Forum masses. I can recall the rhythms of sound at the Forum perfectly: tight silence for long periods, the sudden exhalation of "Oooh!" with the slice and swish of skates, and even the thud of the puck audible throughout the building—and then the sudden explosion of sound when the Habs scored.

Today, the Bell Centre audience cheers, it sings in unison, and everyone wears a red jersey (few wore Canadiens sweaters to the old games). This is the Jarry Park crowd—passionate, hopeful, high-spirited, more accepting of loss—and the Jarry Park rituals, transferred to a new place. It derives from, or repeats unconsciously, the rites and rituals of Expos fandom, with jubilation at just being present. At a moment when Montreal's stature as a second city—a provincial capital like Barcelona or Manchester, proud to be the first city of a subculture—has become accepted, even celebrated, it makes sense that the Canadiens have become the Expos. They are Montreal's soul-team, with close now close enough.

For a long while, I kept all the Expos opening-game ticket stubs as trophies; they're probably still somewhere in our New York apartment. My sister Morgan is now an ocean scientist, with a PhD from Duke University in North Carolina; her husband, Tom, is a government lawyer in Washington, DC. Both are members of what seems to be, to those who belong to it, the vast anglophone diaspora from Montreal. They are devoted Nationals fans, and see the Expos' defection to Washington as a slightly sad but mostly welcome incident in their lives.

I doubt that the Expos are really coming back. But if they do return, I'll be there at the opening game. I imagine a small, perfect ballpark within sight of the Bell Centre; one of those chilly Montreal April afternoons; and, perhaps, in the manner of the new stadiums, local food—smoked meat and poutine—in place of the old park's homogenized hot dogs. I hope to bring my dad, and my sisters, and maybe a child of my own. That other family from the reservoir will show, greyed but ready. We may even, at long last, learn their names.

Access Denied

PAUL HAAVARDSRUD

DON SCOTT IS late. He's supposed to be at a Holiday Inn off Deerfoot Trail, but he might be caught in traffic. Maybe the late spring weather got him. It's a rainy day and Calgary drivers aren't built for wet roads.

It might also be a metaphor. In the 2012 election, Premier Alison Redford vowed to bring the inner workings of Alberta's government into the light. Voters around the world are well used to such campaign-trail rhetoric. Transparency! Accountability! Open government! But changing the culture of an established bureaucracy, not to mention the modus operandi of career politicians, is easier said than done. Redford came out of the blocks running. A month after winning she created a new department, the Ministry of Accountability, Transparency and Transformation. To lead the charge, she tapped Scott, a lawyer and rookie MLA from Fort McMurray-Conklin.

Scott's start, at least on this day, is less auspicious. A handful of people are clumped together in a room full of empty tables, waiting. Scott is halfway through a 12-day provincial tour, part of a review of Alberta's Freedom of Information and Protection of Privacy Act, or FOIP. Most of these sessions are designed for the public, but this one is specifically for journalists. The turnout isn't promising. Four members

61

of the media are here—a pair from Shaw Cable and two from this magazine. An interest group has sent a representative, and a few concerned citizens have come out.

Once Scott arrives, he dutifully delivers his spiel on the FOIP Act review. Other presenters do their bit, questions are fielded, there's some milling around and then it's back out the door and into the rain. All told, Scott's summer barnstorm across Alberta drew about 150 people. The online portion of the FOIP consultation, which lasted roughly six weeks, garnered 400 responses and another 30 written submissions.

In theory, Alberta's disclosure law says government is a caretaker of information that belongs to citizens. In practice, however, those that actually seek information under the FOIP Act—journalists, opposition MLAs, watchdog groups, academics and others invested in keeping tabs on our leaders—say the system also has built-in features that allow for as much obstruction as access.

That politicians can be unscrupulous is, sadly, a given. Conflicts of interest, illegal donations, influence peddling, Mike Duffy and Nigel Wright, Pamela Wallin, Mulroney–Schreiber, Shawinigate—the list goes on. A legislated right to know what takes place behind closed doors can help bring skeletons into the light. Better still, the mere presence of a strong disclosure law can deter corruption before it happens, curbing the number of skeletons hidden in the first place.

The right to know what government is up to is considered a pillar of democracy. The job of upholding democracy, it bears noting, feels out of place amidst the bad coffee and free plastic pens of a Holiday Inn. But if Redford and Scott are sincere in their pledge to openness, public consultation is just the beginning. Much needs to be done to overhaul a FOIP system that stacks the deck in favour of opaqueness.

SECRECY, POWER AND transparency share a long history. The Roman historian Tacitus used the term *arcana imperii* to describe the clandestine approach used by emperors to maintain authority. The idea of *arcana imperii* was taken up by Renaissance philosophers who saw secrecy as a tool used by their own monarchs to consolidate power. The tide began to shift during the Enlightenment. In 1766 Sweden adopted the world's first freedom of information act. Drafted by Anders Chydenius, a learned priest from a hinterlands parish, the law's Swedish name is *offentlighetsprincipen*, or the "principle of publicity." Before Chydenius, any writing about the affairs of Swedish state was banned.

The thinkers who shaped the early days of democracy understood the inherent political tension between transparency and secrecy. In 1822 James Madison, who penned the first drafts of the US Constitution and the Bill of Rights, wrote that "a popular Government, without popular information or the means of acquiring it, is but a Prologue to a Farce or a Tragedy; or, perhaps both. Knowledge will forever govern ignorance: And a people who mean to be their own Governors must arm themselves with the power which knowledge gives."

Access to information in a modern sense is relatively new. The US adopted the Freedom of Information Act in 1966 following years of public pressure. The groundbreaking legislation served as a model for a handful of other countries, which implemented disclosure laws over the next few decades. Canada waited until 1982 to adopt its Access to Information Act. The fall of the Iron Curtain in 1989 saw a spike in the number of freedom of information (FOI) laws on the books. Now, more than 90 countries have some form of disclosure legislation. Among Canadian provinces, Nova Scotia blazed the trail, implementing its Freedom of Information Act in 1977. New Brunswick followed a year later. Alberta didn't adopt its FOIP Act until 1995. That still beat Prince Edward Island, which took until 2002 to proclaim legislation.

Alberta's FOIP Act covers a lot of ground. It deals with protection of privacy: what information can be collected about citizens, who uses it, and for what, and how it can be disclosed. It also grants Albertans the right to information held by public bodies—government ministries, school boards, municipalities, police and others.

In its first General Assembly in 1946, the United Nations called freedom of information a fundamental human right. In 1995 the UN further explained: "Freedom will be bereft of all effectiveness if the people have no access to information. Access to information is basic to the democratic way of life. The tendency to withhold information from the people at large is therefore to be strongly checked."

If governments are indeed hard-wired for secrecy, then freedom-of-information legislation can be thought of as a counterbalance. Information gives citizens the tools to scrutinize government decisions, to know what questions to ask and to make educated decisions at election time.

How does Alberta's FOIP system stack up to other places? Not well. Each year, the media industry association Newspapers Canada issues report cards that compare the quality of disclosure regimes in Canadian jurisdictions. In 2012 Alberta received a B for the speed with which FOIP requests are processed, but a D for its completeness of disclosure—the third-lowest grade in the country. The Centre for Law and Democracy, a non-profit organization based in Halifax, found similar results in its 2012 study, which looks at 61 indicators of transparent regimes. Alberta scored 53 per cent, tying for last place among Canadian provinces and 55th in the world, behind Colombia and Mongolia but just ahead of Angola and Thailand.

"Certainly, I'm not very happy that Alberta's law did as poorly in those studies as it did," says Jill Clayton, Alberta's Information and Privacy commissioner. "I think there's a lot of room to improve." Clayton became Alberta's third privacy commissioner in early 2012. Her job deals with all things FOIP in the province. If a FOIP user feels a request was handled improperly, for instance, the appeal ends up on Clayton's desk. Experts say an empowered official acting at arm's length from government differentiates transparent regimes from more secretive ones.

Alberta having a FOIP Act and a privacy commissioner puts it ahead of places that don't. Legislation, though, only goes so far. "A law is only as good as its implementation," Clayton says. "You can have the strongest law in the world and not have the resources or the political will to implement it properly." Alberta's shortcomings when it comes to freedom of information, as Clayton suggests, can be split into three areas: the legislation itself, how the law is implemented and political will.

No FOI legislation allows citizens access to everything. Some information, whether personal or from a public body, must be confidential. It's easy to understand, for instance, why a person's medical history shouldn't be available to just anyone. Alberta doesn't have nuclear weapon launch codes, but if we ever do, we'd best keep them beyond the reach of a FOIP request. Information laws attempt to balance the competing interests of privacy and availability through a mechanism known as "exceptions to disclosure." Alberta's FOIP Act contains a long list of exceptions. Information may be withheld if it's deemed harmful to public safety, protected by privacy laws or would hurt the business interests of a third party (e.g., terms of contracts signed with government). But exceptions can also be used to keep information hidden from public view, even if doing so violates the spirit of the law.

Alberta's FOIP Act contains an exception, for instance, that allows cabinet ministers to keep all manner of records— briefing materials, meeting minutes, emails—away from the public. The idea is to protect the decision-making process, allowing for frank discussions among officials. What's lacking, though, is an obligation to prove how the information, if disclosed, would harm the public interest. Without such a test, this exception can be used as a catch-all that allows officials to withhold almost any information. The Centre for Law and Democracy is unequivocal in critiquing what Alberta puts out of bounds, noting the province is "one of the worst jurisdictions in the world with regards to its treatment of exceptions. Together, these loopholes ensure that the law cannot serve as a proper tool of governmental accountability, as they provide an enormous amount of wiggle room for recalcitrant public officials who would seek to avoid disclosure of embarrassing information."

Alberta's FOIP Act may also be overridden by so-called paramountcy provisions contained in other legislation. Such clauses carve chunks out of the FOIP Act, putting information beyond its reach. Alberta's law is trumped by more than 35 paramountcy provisions. The Mines and Minerals Act, for example, contains a clause that excises information about royalties from the disclosure law. The rationale behind the exclusion is to protect the competitive interests of oil and gas companies. The clause, though, also prevents Albertans from gaining insight into the billions in royalty dollars collected each year from resources they ostensibly own. Throw enough paramountcy provisions at a law and experts say even the best legislation will be effectively neutered.

In his review of the legislation, Scott says everything is on the table, including exemptions from the Act. "We're going to be looking at each exemption," says Scott. "We're asking: Does it make sense for Albertans?" Scott has enlisted five experts on freedom of information to help, in part by examining policy elsewhere. Once finished, Scott says, this province's legislation will measure up to any in the world. Not everyone is as hopeful. Laurie Blakeman, MLA for Edmonton-Centre and Liberal opposition house leader, is particularly skeptical of Scott's promise. In 2010 she joined an all-party committee that presented 24 recommendations to the legislature following a nearly year-long review of the FOIP Act. None were acted upon. "Now we have a new minister doing a new review," Blakeman says. "When I asked him, 'Explain to me why you would repeat this effort all over again,' he couldn't."

Scott has heard the knocks on his legislative review, as well as the criticisms about Alberta's approach to disclosure. He disagrees with both. "I'm certainly aware that some people think there's a culture of secrecy [in Alberta's government]," he says. "My own experience with this government, and even with this FOIP review process, is that we're getting information out."

For Scott's new legislation to become law, he'll still need to get a bill past cabinet and his colleagues in the legislature. Even if that happens, the work still won't be finished.

Finding the political will to properly implement the law is another matter entirely.

THE EXPERIENCE OF using FOIP in Alberta is seldom described as user-friendly. "I can buy rare Belgian beers online with a credit card and have them in my house 24 hours later, yet I can't make a FOIP request to my own provincial government without a pile of paperwork and pulling out cheques," says Scott Hennig, a vice president at the Canadian Taxpayers Federation (CTF). "I'll be the only guy buying stamps and cheques when I'm 80, because they don't want to make this any easier on us. And if they could...figure out how I'd have to go hand-deliver a stone tablet, they would."

Alberta levies a $25 charge for each FOIP request, a cost that may seem small, but one that Hennig says can deter potential filers. Some Canadian jurisdictions charge only $5 per request. Across the country, the CTF files upwards of 500 FOI requests a year. Whether governments should even charge to process FOI requests is open to debate. Hennig has discussed many of his concerns with Scott and is hopeful about the review. That said, he also wonders how a bureaucratic culture that's taken an oppositional approach to information requests for so long might actually change. "We fill out a request, we send it and we basically plead with a public body to provide us with information, whereas we should be viewing it as no different than our right to vote," says Hennig. "We don't go to the polls and plead with the election worker to please allow us a ballot so we might vote, and then they have a decision to make on whether they're going to give us one or not."

A REQUEST FOR information begins by contacting the FOIP officer at a public body. The City of Red Deer has one, as does Alberta's Ministry of Energy, Alberta Health Services and the Edmonton Police. Alberta has 903 FOIP coordinators in all. Sometimes information is sought from a big department that handles hundreds of requests a year, such as Alberta Environment. In other cases, "FOIP coordinator" is only one hat worn by a staffer in a municipal office that rarely sees a request.

Having hundreds of coordinators using individual discretion to interpret legislation, handle requests and redact documents would seem to jeopardize consistent application of the law. But regular FOIP users are generous in describing the work done by coordinators, saying most believe in the spirit of the law and do their best to get information out as quickly as resources allow. The more serious problems with FOIP often reside further up the food chain. For information to be truly free, the powers that be have to want it that way. In theory, FOIP staff are independent from the departments in which they work. In reality, political interference still happens.

Frank Work spent a decade as Alberta's Information and Privacy Commissioner. Before leaving in 2011, Work saw FOIP requests stymied in any number of ways. "You can have a really good law, but human ingenuity being what it is, if there's not the willingness to implement it, there are always ways to circumvent it. There are always ways to slow it down and delay it," he says. "I defy anyone to come up with a law that will force good access to information on a public body that doesn't want to do it."

For a FOIP user, what happens behind the curtain is a black box. Once a request form is dropped in the mail, power shifts to the recipient. The system may well work as planned—a FOIP coordinator gets a request, finds the information and sends it out. Given higher stakes, though,

Work says the flow of information can slow to a trickle, a tactic that can frustrate or even derail requests. Some deputy or assistant deputy ministers will even review requests that could be politically damaging, be it a conflict of interest or improper spending on the taxpayer's dime. If a piece of information makes someone in charge uncomfortable, frontline staff are unlikely to pass it along anytime soon.

Legislation sets a 30-day window to respond to requests following which a public body can ask for a 30-day extension. Once 60 days have passed, a department head may choose to withhold information by, for example, applying an overly broad interpretation to an exception. They must provide a reason for denying information, and the decision can be appealed to the privacy commissioner. Still, the bureaucratic back-and-forth doesn't happen quickly. "A public body can refuse to give the time of day if it wanted to and that would force [a request] to wind up at the commissioner's office," says Work. "That would…add a year, two years, maybe even more to the process." If information is time-sensitive and concerns, say, something that would be material to an election, stalling can effectively defang a request.

Delaying is only one tactic used to avoid disclosure. Cost is another. Beyond the initial $25 charge, processing fees can run into the thousands and even tens of thousands of dollars. The privacy commissioner can be asked to waive the cost on the grounds of public interest. These requests will sometimes be granted, but the experience of churning through the process is, once again, both frustrating and time-consuming.

Most Albertans will never file a FOIP request, but for those who do, the byzantine workings of government prove another hurdle to accessing information. Without an intimate knowledge of the type of information that exists, it can be hard to even know where to begin.

Pick something you'd like to know more about. Maybe you're from Cold Lake and you're curious about the oil that seeped out of Canadian Natural Resources Ltd.'s Primrose project last year. Maybe you want to know what CNRL told government. How do you start? Which department do you approach? What information do you want to find out? What questions do you ask? What wording do you use in your request? Have you a right to government email exchanges with CNRL executives? If the FOIP coordinator delivers a fee estimate that runs into the thousands of dollars, what then? And if you eventually get a box full of blacked-out papers, what recourse do you have?

CHARLES RUSNELL HAS spent a career answering these types of questions. An investigative reporter with CBC Edmonton, he made his first FOI request in 1984 while still in journalism school. Since then he's filed thousands more. (Full disclosure: Rusnell is a colleague at CBC.)

At any given time, Rusnell and his investigative partner, Jennie Russell, have several hundred requests on the go. They used FOIP to help break news that forced the dismissal of former AHS chief financial officer Allaudin Merali, whose expense report left citizens on the hook for hundreds of thousands of dollars in questionable claims. Their requests also informed the public that Premier Redford, when she was justice minister, took part in the decision to award a government tobacco-litigation contract—the largest legal action in Alberta's history—to her ex-husband's firm. Other conflicts of interest brought to light include those of Edmonton-Manning MLA Peter Sandhu, who lobbied ministers and government officials to change legislation that would benefit his struggling homebuilding company. Such success shows that Alberta's FOIP system can work. That said, Rusnell and Russell spent years developing the institutional knowledge needed to navigate a system that can set people up to fail. "What we see every day in our work is still, within the government, a resistance and an unwillingness to be transparent," Rusnell says. "What many of them don't understand—or they don't care to understand—is that they don't own this information. It belongs to the public, we have a right to it. They're simply the ones who keep the information for us."

Rusnell seems alternately weary of the barriers he has to negotiate and angry that those roadblocks even exist. Part of the problem, he says, comes back to resources. "We talk to freedom of information coordinators all the time and I don't give them a hard time about not meeting deadlines. They're swamped," he says. "They have so much work and they're not properly funded." Many departments, Rusnell says, believe in the spirit of the law and work hard to get information out. A lack of resources, though, is in itself a built-in obstruction to disclosure. A FOIP coordinator may need to dig through a patchwork of storage boxes, filing cabinets and computer systems to find answers. If Redford's government is serious about transparency, it would commit to digitizing files and making databases easier to search. This would take resolve, but it would also lay the groundwork for more proactive disclosure and a truly open government.

As things stand, Albertans must make do with a status quo that puts the onus of keeping government honest on the shoulders of a few watchful groups. Michael Geist, a law professor at the University of Ottawa, is on the panel advising Scott's review. Any scrutiny of access to information regimes, he notes, also puts into relief the customary role of the press as the fourth estate. "You need heavy, knowledgeable users who can use the system to bring greater transparency to the activities of governments...but we don't need everyone using it all the time," Geist says. "We don't get everybody showing up to a press conference to ask the questions they have of an elected official. The media does it and then spreads the word." The decline of traditional media in the revenue-crumbling age of online news augurs poorly for government accountability in Alberta. The CBC's Rusnell and Russell may be doing yeoman's work, but beyond them, few, if any, journalists in the province have the time or resources to make more than haphazard use of FOIP requests. The *Calgary Herald* and the *Edmonton Journal*, to name just two outlets, are shells of their former selves, both newsrooms gutted of copy editors, reporters and senior writers.

THOMAS JEFFERSON IS credited with saying the price of freedom is eternal vigilance. No matter how pleasant life is in Alberta—an affluent province nestled inside one of the world's most democratic countries—it would seem unwise to become complacent about the laws that safeguard that comfort. When the virtues and pitfalls of democracy were still being mapped, thinkers such as Jefferson and Madison saw the power imbalance that arises when a select few know more than everyone else. When citizens place their faith in a democratic government, they accept this inequality; the right to information is government's way of returning that trust. Decisions made in secret can be arbitrary or even corrupt. If no one knows, who's to find out?

Don Scott hopes to complete his FOIP review and have new legislation in front of the house for the spring session. If not, he says, fall at the latest. A cynic could see his tardy arrival to the Holiday Inn back in the spring as a poor omen. Rather than overhauling vital legislation, the review may only be ticking the box on his boss' campaign promise. Albertans, for their part, should hope he was just caught in traffic.

The Reverse

JESSAMYN HOPE

3:30

"TODAY'S THE DAY," said Andrea, my diving coach, standing with her thick legs apart, back arched, meaty arms crossed over her large bosom. "Today's the goddamn day."

I nodded. My crotch tingled as if I needed to pee, but I knew that was impossible. Before leaving the locker room, I had balanced over the toilet three times, the last time unable to squeeze out a single drop of fear.

Andrea squinted at the bleachers on the other side of the indoor swimming pool, where my friend Theresa sat like a small sun, her light-blond bangs shooting ten centimetres into the air and fanning open. To achieve this gravity-defying look Theresa would soak her bangs in hairspray and then press them, panini-style, between two books. The rest of her hair fell softly to her shoulders, framing her small, vulpine face, which was twisting around a jawbreaker. Without the bangs, scrawny Theresa barely made five feet.

Andrea ran her hand through her short, russety hair and said, "What is that punk doing here again? Does she have a crush on you? Tell your lesbo friend to take off."

"She's not a lesbian," I said, having only a vague idea of what a lesbian was and no idea of what a lesbian did. Actually, my sole image of a lesbian was Andrea, because that's what one of the older divers had called her last week, the same boy who, to my utter bafflement, always called Greg Louganis "Greg Loose-Anus."

Andrea clapped her hands and pointed at me between the eyes. "Listen, my little Star of David, if you don't do the reverse dive today, you're out. Off the team! You've been wriggling your way out of it for months. If you don't do the dive by"—Andrea looked toward the big round clock hanging high on the cement wall—"four o'clock, that's it. You can walk your coward's ass on out of here, clean out your locker, and never show your face at this pool again."

3:36

I TOOK MY time going through the warm-up exercises on the blue gym mats to the left of the boards. I grimaced through twenty lunges and fifteen push-ups. While doing my sixty sit-ups, I pictured how nice it was going to be two hours from now—diving practice behind me, Theresa and I down at the shops, eating poutine out of Styrofoam containers, a full twenty-two hours to go before I had to be at the pool again.

The Pointe-Claire municipal pool had no windows, yet somehow a sense of the January outside—already dark at this early hour and twenty-five below—mingled with the smell of chlorine. Under a very steep, church-like roof, high enough to accommodate a ten-metre diving platform, lay Canada's first Olympic-sized swimming pool, built in 1967. Twenty-one years later, this was still the training ground for the country's best swimming and diving team, and a number of Olympic medalists and World Record holders were diving off its boards that very afternoon. All around me were strong, beautiful bodies: practicing handstands, somersaulting high above the trampoline, bounding off the springboards and soaring into the air as if they had a different relationship with gravity, seeming to suspend a moment, arms spread open, before falling toward the water straight as a spear. After emerging from the pool, wet and glistening, they would grab their pastel shammies and whip each other's bums, joking and laughing as if we were doing something fun here.

I lay back on the blue mat and stared up at the roof's crisscrossing rafters. That I would sooner or later have to do a reverse dive—where a diver jumps off the board facing forward, but then flips backward, toward the board—had been haunting me for over a year. When I set off for my first diving practice, my dad said he was allowing me take up the sport on one condition: that I never, ever do a reverse dive, which in his South African English accent he called "a gainer." To make doubly sure I obeyed, he claimed that on any summer day, half the people in an emergency room were there thanks to gainers.

Why was Dad so alarmist about reverse dives? Probably because five years earlier in Edmonton, a diver from the Soviet Union named Sergei Chalibashvili smacked his head while doing a reverse dive and died. I was too young to remember the accident, but it must have been in all the Canadian papers because Chalibashvili, to this day, is the only diver to be killed during an international competition. What happened after the medics carried Chalibashvili away is diving lore: Greg Louganis, who'd been standing on the ten-metre platform when Chalibashvili's head hit it, after peeking over the edge and seeing the water filled with blood, had to go ahead and do the exact same dive—a reverse with three-and-a-half somersaults—a dive Louganis himself had hit his head doing a few years earlier in Tbilisi, USSR, which just happened to be Chalibashvili's hometown.

I had recently seen the video of Louganis hitting his head back in 1979 in Tbilisi. They had replayed it on TV that past October after he once again hit his head doing a reverse at the Summer Games in Seoul. If I hadn't already been terrified of the dive, I would have been after seeing that old black-and-white footage. It came to me again as I lay on the blue mat, Louganis smashing his skull against the hard platform and then, head joggling as if he were a bobblehead doll, losing consciousness in midair and just falling, limply falling, until he met the water with a flat back.

"Hey there, Sleeping Beauty." Andrea's ruddy face stared down at me. She was bent over, hands on her knees, the roof sloping up behind her. "Would you like a pillow?"

3:41

MY FIRST WARM-UP dive—a simple front dive from the one-metre—did not go well.

"Like piss hitting a plate," Andrea said as I pushed out of the pool. She was leaning back in her steel fold-up chair, one ankle resting on her knee, her hands propped on her wide waist.

I grabbed my blue shammy off the bleacher and wiped down my arms and legs.

Eyeing my white thighs, Andrea said, "You're not the skinnymalink you were a few months ago. You're getting boobs and hips, eh? Too bad. Harder to slice the water like a knife when you've got bags of fat hanging off you. Not impossible, but harder."

I nodded as if I were to blame for the new breasts pushing against the plasticky white windmill on the front of my swimsuit. The team emblem was the Pointe-Claire Windmill, "the oldest windmill in Montreal," built by Sulpician priests in 1709, when the only other people leaving snow prints on this part of the island were the Iroquois. That was hundreds of years before the land became a suburb of the city, covered in track homes and strip malls, and more than 250 years before my parents would immigrate to Canada, but it never occurred to me that this windmill wasn't a part of my history. I was very proud of that team swimsuit. The first time I put it on, I stood in front of my bedroom mirror, hands down at my sides, chin raised like a soldier at attention, thinking, Look at that, you're an athlete now.

Back in line for the board, I waited behind Jackie, a buck-toothed girl who was, it could not be denied, a truly good diver now. When the two of us first made the team, I had been a far better diver. I had been the best of all the rookies. Until recently I had always been the best at whatever I did: the fastest runner on the street, the highest climber of trees, the top student in Greendale Elementary. I had played Snow White in a production downtown, singing and dancing for an audience of hundreds while an understudy almost twice my age waited in the wings. But lately, everything had become a lot harder. My last report card, hidden under my mattress since the summer, had been a column of Cs. My parents were too preoccupied, first fighting over Dad's friendship with his new secretary, then driving Mom back and forth to the Royal Vic for "treatments," to notice that I never gave it to them. Six months later I was still debating whether I had moral obligation to bring the shameful report card to their attention. The director of my drama school, after failing to give me a lead role in *West Side Story*, asked, "Whatever happened, Jessamyn, to your beautiful voice?" And all the other new divers had gotten better, executing dives with higher and higher degrees of difficulty, while my dives stayed the same, leaving me the worst diver on the team.

I have to do this dive today, I thought. I have to do it. It would be proof that I wasn't going to be a failure from here on out, that I wasn't going to be the remarkable little girl who grew up to be a big sad disappointment, that I was still on track to be a remarkable woman, the kind of woman who didn't let fear stand in her way. If I didn't do this dive, I would officially be a coward. Never to do anything great. Never to be admired. Or loved, not truly loved, the way Gilbert Blythe loved Anne Shirley. Gilbert never would've been so taken by Anne, yearning for her year after year, if she hadn't been the bravest and most talented girl he had ever met. This was my last chance to prove that I was an Anne of Green Gables, Jo March, Scarlett O'Hara.

3:47

AFTER MESSING UP another front dive, I swam for the pool's edge without coming up for air. The world above was a muffled blur. As long as I was underwater, everything was on hold.

Andrea pretended I was invisible when I climbed out of the pool, looking all around except at me, as if my dive had been too terrible to be real.

I got back in line for the board, teeth chattering. Squeezing the water out of my black braid, I peeked up at the clock. Thirteen more minutes. Maybe I really did have to pee now?

I looked over at Theresa, still sitting on the bleacher, chewing her jawbreaker. Catching my eyes on her, she lifted her small hand and turned up her small mouth. I smiled back, thinking, Why? Why did she come with me, every afternoon, across the slushy boulevard from our high school to the pool? I knew Theresa was needy, everybody knew it, there wasn't a girl in our grade Theresa hadn't dragged into a photobooth, as if she required photographic evidence that she had friends. Still, lonely or not, how could she stand it, sitting on that bleacher, day after day, watching other kids work hard to get good at something? Didn't it bother her that she wasn't good at anything?

When I first started spending my evenings with Theresa, hanging at the shops and staying late at her townhouse, often sleeping over since Theresa lived around the corner from our high school, my mom didn't like it. She said, "Theresa's mom's never home. All you eat there are microwaved hotdogs"—a comment so out of character for my mother, a woman who made Toblerone fondue for dinner, that it still niggles at me decades later. My mother was an Italian immigrant, a stay-at-home mom, but she never said conventional "mom" things, never scrunched her nose at other women and their homes, and there's just something about that microwaved-hotdog comment that I can't quite put my finger on.

Mom didn't press the point, though. How could she, when we weren't eating much better at home? Not since the breast cancer came back for the third time, and Mom and Dad finally told me about the other two times, because this time was guaranteed to be the last. If Mom wasn't at the hospital, she was either sitting in the family room on the puffy black recliner, wearing her oversized auburn wig, a neck brace, and a scowl, or she was locked in her bedroom with the silver vomit dish, mostly in silence, though once I heard her cry out: "Please, dear God, just kill me already!" As for Theresa's mom, I had no idea where she was. I never asked. I just made the most of her absence.

A full year of school nights at Theresa's townhouse, and all I'm left with now are a few flashes: my hands bringing a plate of frozen hotdogs up to the microwave; Theresa cackling as she pulled a strand of condoms out of her mother's half-packed suitcase; sitting cross-legged on the beige carpet, passing the telephone back and forth while we talked on the Party Line to "Nine-Inch Brian," whom Theresa told, unable to suppress her cackle, that we were Catholic schoolgirls.

Who would have thought that an adult man would desire a schoolgirl? But Theresa knew things at a time, in those last years before the Internet, when it wasn't so easy to find things out. It wasn't a prudish era; sex was everywhere—Calvin Klein ads, slapstick comedies, music videos (George Michael wanted yours)—but exactly what everybody was talking about could remain, sometimes for years, unclear, a little fuzzy, like those scrambled soft-core movies that came on after midnight. Only Theresa, between her "fuck this" and "fuck that," bandied about terms like *blowjob* and *rimmer* and *double-team* like she totally knew what they meant, always followed by her machine-gun HA HA HA HA HA!

That's why it was such a surprise when, earlier that year, in the middle of Sex Ed, while we were watching a close-up of a baby's hairy head pushing out of a stretched vagina, Theresa fainted. She timbered out of her chair—the shadow of her spiky bangs passing over the screen—and landed with a crash in front of the film projector.

3:50

"SHOW TIME!" ANDREA said, when I popped my head out of the water after finally doing a decent front dive. "Time to shine, Star of David."

I looked to the clock. "You said I had until four!"

"Jessamyn!"

"Please," I begged, clasping the side of the pool. "Can't I do a few more warm-up dives?"

"One more," Andrea said, holding a finger up in front of her face as if I didn't know what one meant.

I glanced back at Theresa who shook her head like "fuck that." Andrea followed my eyes and ordered me to go tell my loser friend to get lost.

I said, "I won't look at her again, I promise."

"She's creepy. Tell her to go home."

I walked around the pool, hunched, arms twisted in front of my chest. Instead of walking around the boards, I took the long way, circumnavigating the swimming lanes with their furious back and forth of goggled swimmers. At the far end of the pool, I paused to watch Katherine, only one year older than me, all the way up on the ten-metre platform, standing still, mentally preparing for her dive. When she started to run, my chest rose and the breath caught in my throat. She leapt off the platform with her arms above her head, whipped them forward, and started falling while spinning, not in a ball, but bent in two at the waist, arms wrapped around her straight legs, going round and round, and opening up just in time to pierce the water. I exhaled, and thought about how good it must feel to be a work of art.

"Coach says you have to go."

Theresa's eyes were as blue and clear as the pool. Judging by her tongue and lips, her jawbreaker had been blue too.

"Bitch," Theresa said. "I still don't get why she keeps calling you Star of David. Who the fuck is David?"

"Seriously, you have to leave right now."

"You don't have to do it, you know."

"Yeah, I do. You need a reverse to compete."

"Why do you have to compete?"

"Because that's what it means to do a sport, Theresa," I said, although I knew that I no longer had to do the reverse to compete. I had to do it to quit. Do this one last dive, and I could walk away with dignity. "I told you, I have to push myself."

"Why do you have to push yourself?"

I glanced back at Andrea who opened her hands in a 'What's taking so long?' gesture.

Turning back to Theresa, I said, "Honestly, I don't know why I hang out with you."

"Fuck you!" Theresa said with a cackle-laugh and picked up her army backpack. "I'll wait for you in the foyer."

As I walked back around the pool, again the long way, again hunched with my arms folded in front of my chest, a doughnut popped into my head—a soft white yeasty doughnut topped with chocolate icing and pink and blue sprinkles. Without fail, this doughnut came to me every practice. I could see it, smell it, almost taste it. The vision of this doughnut, sitting on a piece of wax paper on a red counter in front of a giant mirror bordered by vanity lights, was at once ironclad and hazy, as first memories tend to be. When I was four years old and taking swimming lessons at the indoor pool closer to our house in Dollard-des-Ormeaux, my mom would buy me a doughnut to eat afterward, and this doughnut was in the locker room waiting for me to finish changing into dry clothes. Cavernous indoor pool, fear of drowning, followed by a doughnut.

3:57

UPON MY RETURN, Andrea said, "That took too long. No more warm-up dives."

I looked to the clock. "You said I had until four!"

"Jesus Christ, Jessamyn! Have some mercy on me."

"You said I had until four."

"By the time you're on the board, it'll be four."

3:58

JACKIE CLIMBED ONTO the green springboard, and I moved to next in line. One year younger than me, Jackie still had her childhood body. She adjusted the fulcrum, moving the knob back with her pale foot and spindly leg.

Crossing my legs against the pee feeling, I ran through the reverse in my head, because that was what all the great athletes said you should do. Never think while moving, they said. Imagine yourself doing the perfect dive (or dunk or catch or whatever) over and over again, so that when the time comes, your body just does it, automatically, with grace.

I'm standing in the middle of the board, facing the pool. I take the first step of the three-step hurdle. The second step, the third. I jump onto both feet at the end of the board and, as it's bowing beneath me, I bend my knees and jump as it springs back, jump high, not out, and when I'm as high as I'll go, no sooner, I open my arms while looking back...

But if I did as I was supposed to, and only thought about jumping high off the board, not away from it, how was I supposed to make sure I didn't hit my head? And if those great athletes were right, that you'll naturally do what you've been imagining, then what was going to happen after I've been imagining smacking my head all day?

3:59

JACKIE STOOD AT the end of the board, her back to the pool as if she were going to do a back dive, but she was preparing to do an inward, where a diver jumps backward and then flips inward, toward the board. Her pale, freckled face was stern, her big blue eyes focussed. Her long black lashes were in wet, doll-like clumps. Jackie would have been one of the prettiest girls on the team if not for the gigantic buck-teeth that prevented her from ever fully closing her mouth.

When she raised her hands above her head, I thought, oh god, here we go. In two seconds, she'll be done, and I'm up. Jackie jumped, whipped her hands forward, somersaulted in a fast tight tuck, and opened up—

I gasped. Andrea did too.

Jackie's face met the board. She didn't skim her forehead. Her entire face smashed into the board, flat down. The board bent under the pressure and lobbed Jackie off, in an arc, blood sputtering off her face like a summer sprinkler. She landed on her back, the water swallowing her and blooming red.

It felt as if I had wished this on her, as if my imaginings had been that powerful. And yet, that wasn't why I felt so guilty. No, the guilt came with the sweet giddy relief, the weightless tingly sense of good fortune. Now I wouldn't have to do the reverse. Maybe tomorrow, but not today.

"Call 9-1-1!" Andrea shouted as she ran and dove into the water. She surfaced with Jackie and sidestroked back with her under her arm. Jackie fumbled for the steel ladder—at least she was conscious. After managing to climb a rung, Jackie stopped, opened her mouth, and the blood waterfalled out. All of her ugly teeth were gone.

A lifeguard pressed a towel against Jackie's mouth, while another lifeguard, wrapping a towel around her shoulders, said, "You're okay, you're okay, you're okay."

"An ambulance is on the way," came a cry from across the pool.

Everyone stood and watched, from the deck, the one-metre boards, the three-metres, the seven, and the ten, as the lifeguards escorted Jackie out.

4:14

"Okay, your reverse," Andrea said, towelling off her hair.

I widened my eyes at her.

The rest of the divers, after respectfully waiting for Jackie to disappear into the locker room, had gone back to work. The blood had dissipated into the giant pool, been disinfected by the chlorine. The place was loud again with the thud of boards and the swimming coaches' impatient whistles.

Andrea said, "If you don't do it now, you'll never do it. It's a falling off the horse sort of thing."

Louganis after Chalibashvili.

This had become an even bigger test of my heroism.

"Go on," Andrea said. "The longer you wait, the scarier it's going to be."

I turned from Andrea and walked toward the board. I climbed its ladder with my heart pounding hard and fast. No urge to pee. I hardly felt my body. Only the thudding heart. How was I going to control my body if I couldn't feel it?

"Hey!" Andrea said, approaching the side of the board with her hands held high, making a triangle with her thumbs and forefingers.

I made the same triangle but upside-down, and we brought our triangles together.

She said, "Star of David! Powers activate!"

Andrea forced me to do this ritual she had invented every time I was attempting a new or difficult dive. Was she laughing at my being a Jew? Maybe a little. But mostly, I think, she was trying to give me a laugh and wish me good luck. Whenever she said it, I thought of this gold pendant Dad used to wear, a rather large, slanted Star of David that nestled in his chest hair while we played in the swimming pools of Daytona. My favourite game was "The Rocket," where Dad would crouch underwater and I would climb onto his shoulders and he would spring up and I would go rocketing into the air. That was back when I wore a Wonder Woman swimsuit and Mom still had hair, dyed-red, carefully curled hair, which is why she would only wade around in the shallow end, careful to keep her head above the water and out of the way of The Rocket. But I always assumed she was watching me soar into the air, thinking, My daughter, such a daredevil!

Andrea stepped back. I took my position in the middle of the board. I brought my feet together, straightened my back, and lowered my hands by my sides.

4:16

"ONE!" SHOUTED ANDREA when minutes later I was still standing in place.

I didn't turn to look at her. I stayed in position, eyes forward, but she haunted my peripheral vision with her hands cupped around her mouth.

"TWO! If I get to ten and you still haven't done it, that's it! You're done!"

What was she doing? How was I supposed to concentrate with her yelling like that?

"THREE!"

Her voice boomed everything else into silence. The thud of the boards ceased again. I tried not to look, but my eyes leapt about against my will. Everyone, the Olympic hopefuls and medalists, the other coaches, the newbies who were far better than me now, had all stopped to watch. Even a few swimmers had gathered to the right of my board.

"FOUR!"

You have to do this, I thought. You have to do it. Do it.

"FIVE!"

The doughnut. What? Why the doughnut now!

"SIX!"

I knew what those great athletes meant by not thinking, I really did. Once I had been able to do it, to simply be, simply move, trust, trust that things were going to be fine, better than fine, good, perfect, but now I couldn't get my mind to shut up to shut up to shut up just shut up and go go go

"SEVEN!"

Go go go go go go go

"EIGHT!"

Oh my god, oh my god, I'm going. I'm going! Look, my bare foot taking the first step.

"NINE!"

The second step, oh oh am I really doing this, the third step, I'm still not sure, I'm jumping onto both feet at the end of the board, bending my legs, and—

There I remained. Frozen. On bent knees. The very picture of a cower.

Andrea didn't bother with "Ten." Everyone watched as I straightened my legs, but not my shoulders, turned around, and made my way back down the board.

Andrea shook her head. "Go pack your stuff."

4:33

ALONE IN THE communal showers, under a jet of hot water, I stood for a long time, half hoping Andrea would come and tell me that it was okay, she was just trying to play hard ball, I was still on the team, and half hoping I would never lay eyes on her again. It dawned on me that I was in the middle of a second test, that Andrea was out there right now, standing by the board, waiting to see if I would come back and beg for a second chance to prove myself.

5:00

OUT IN THE foyer, Theresa looked up from her paperback copy of *Cujo*.

She asked, "Did you do it?"

I shook my head. My backpack was filled with all the things I wouldn't be needing anymore: Ultraswim shampoo, the shammy, the swimsuit with the iron-on windmill.

"Good," Theresa said, slipping her arm through mine.

I shoved her arm away and pushed through the glass doors into the wintery night. Since it was considered nerdy to acknowledge the cold, neither one of us wore hats, mitts, or boots, just acid-wash jean jackets, Theresa's hanging off her shoulders, and Converse high-tops. In seconds my wet hair would harden into Medusa-like icicles.

The sidewalk in front of the building was lined with cars, parents waiting in the drivers' seats, headlights on. My mom's face used to wait for me behind the windshield of an old boxy white Buick—her high, plump cheeks, thin lips, green angora beret over her red hair, black winged eyeliner magnifying her already big, black eyes. I could always tell when her eyes caught sight of me coming toward the car. She didn't smile or wave, but she just looked happier, reanimated, as she turned the key on the engine. I would climb into the heated Buick and Billy Joel would sing us down Saint John's Boulevard, past the big shopping centre and fast food huts. If we didn't pick up Harvey's or McDonald's on the way home, she would make a huge bowl of her chunky french fries with the skins still on, which I would soak in salt and vinegar and eat sitting on the brown carpet behind the coffee table, watching *Today's Special,* followed by *The Cosby Show, Family Ties, Cheers, Night Court.* There were no quotas on TV in our house.

And it hits me, not then, but today, thirty years later. Thirty years too late. I'm lying on my side in bed, my husband asleep behind me, and I'm nodding off after a day spent writing out this memory—the reverse, the reverse—when my eyes pop open. I clutch the comforter and stare into the darkness of the bedroom, a dark bedroom in New York City, so far away from there, from then, from that autumn morning Mom stood in the sunlit foyer in her red velvet housecoat and, watching me put on my jean jacket, asked whether I was planning to go to Theresa's again after diving. Mom probably no longer filled out the red housecoat; it probably hung on hunched, bony shoulders. She probably no longer filled out her face, but I can't say for sure because I wouldn't look at her face, at those harrowed black eyes. She said, "I don't like it. All you eat there are microwaved hotdogs," as I walked out the door. No wonder those words wouldn't go away. How could I have been so slow? Knowing she had only a few months left with her daughter, Mom was saying, hey, instead of going to Theresa's every night, I would really like it if you came home. But she couldn't say that, knowing the whole reason I wasn't coming home was because she was there, dying.

Theresa said, "Hey, Jess. You have no reason to be mad at me. I didn't do anything. I didn't kick you off the team."

Theresa was right, so I nodded, but I still couldn't look at her. We crossed the snowy parking lot, its street lamps throwing small circles of light on the compacted snow. Empty white spotlights. The grief was breathtaking. Not for Mom yet, but for me.

I was gone.

I Hope I'm Old Before I Die

GREG HUDSON

START WITH THE accident. Only, it wasn't an accident in the frightening, possibly fatal sense. Although it did happen in a car, and it certainly wasn't intentional.

AROUND CHRISTMAS, I pulled into a gas station to pick up my morning energy drink. I drink at least one every day, usually two. Never as many as four. I don't drink coffee. I was maybe not fully awake, though I can't really list that as even a half-hearted excuse, since a) I was still driving, and b) it's not as though I was up before dawn.

I took my foot off the gas and turned into the parking spot at the side of the building. Then I got confused.

In that moment, I forgot which pedal I had just taken my foot off of. I blanked on which pedal was for stopping and which was for going. Instinctively, I moved my foot to the left, but I was suddenly certain I was wrong, and that if I pushed down, I'd lurch headlong into the side of the Mac's.

It's knowledge that's as familiar as tying my shoe that I've exercised without much thought since I was 16, but that morning it got muddled and slippery. I was lost, as if the number of pedals had doubled, and any one I pressed would lead to me smashing my parents' Astro van into a building.

And in the end, that's what happened. Though, I can't

exaggerate, I was going 10 km/hr max. There was no damage to the wall or my family's van. But it was unnerving. I experienced my first Senior Moment. The real-world result of having the brain of a someone in their 50s.

Which, fine, but I'm only 30 years old.

LAST SUMMER, I went to an age management clinic. I was turning 30, and wasn't happy about it, the same way most people over, say, 29 aren't happy about their birthdays. Maybe I was a little more upset than most people, but that's impossible to know. Mortality—and its inherent deadline for success and satisfaction—is a scary thing. That's why places like the DeerFields Clinic exist.

Only, there aren't many places like DeerFields Clinic. It sits on a converted ranch outside of Toronto and has the relaxed aura of a sanitarium from the 1900s. If that sounds ominous, it's not supposed to. The grounds, the stables, the homey accommodations, the spa and even the medical offices tucked in the basement underneath the small restaurant, practically sigh. It's a place to rest, with horses and free-range food. A place to—if not be reborn—at least de-age.

"Don't talk about the grounds," Dawn Pentesco tells me the first time I go there. She's the marketing woman showing me around like a proud parent. "Whenever people come here, they get distracted by the accommodations, by everything we have here, and how it looks, but they don't talk about what we actually do."

What they do, at least what they'll do for me, is discover my physiological age, as compared to my chronological age. Then, with that knowledge, they make life plans for their clients that involve exercise, diet, supplements and hormone therapy to help reverse the aging process. According to the man in charge, Dr. Randy Knipping, their work can make people at least 11 years younger. That's the work that has been peer reviewed and published, anyway. A 50-year-old can, physiologically, become 39.

"Imagine a classroom of 10-year-olds," Dr. Knipping tells me. "At about that age, everyone is basically at the same age, biologically speaking. After that, lifestyle, disease, genetics, diet all start to change things. When that same group is in their twenties, some will seem younger and others will be living harder."

Knipping uses biomarkers of physiological function to determine your true age. These are things like your lung strength, your circulatory health, your brain power, your endocrine and immune system, your skin and, especially, your telomeres. "If there is one candidate to be considered the body's molecular clock, one of the frontrunners must be the length of our telomeres," the hefty package they sent me home with explains. "Telomeres are the caps on the ends of each of our chromosomes that protect them from being mistaken for damaged DNA." As our cells divide, these ends deplete—like how the tips of shoelaces wear out with each tie. Once they deplete past a certain point, they fail to perform their function and "produce detrimental inflammatory molecules. The molecular clock stops ticking," the literature says. One of the major treatments DeerFields offers is a way to stop the wearing down of these telomeres.

While it takes at least two visits to see exactly how well your body is aging—one visit to get a baseline and another a year later for comparison—I took all the tests in order to get a snapshot of where my body was at.

It wasn't great.

SOME MEDICAL HISTORY:

When I was a teenager, I used to say that I hoped I'd get

asthma, mono or diabetes. To me, these were diseases that offered sympathy, attention and the ability to get out of doing things without any serious consequences, like death. You get a lot of attention if you get lupus, but then you have lupus.

My wish came true when I was diagnosed with diabetes in grade 12. Unfortunately, my diabetes never moved much past a punchline. After diagnosis, I was sent to a three-day tutorial on how to manage my condition. During one discussion about meal plans and what foods I could and couldn't eat, I started to feel overwhelmed by how much my life needed to be controlled, and how much it would change. Then I thought, "Wait, I don't actually have to do any of this." And I felt better instantly.

The problem with my diabetes, since I don't have the type 1, *Steel Magnolias* variety, is that it has no immediate repercussions. If I neglect to take my insulin and my blood sugar skyrockets, I don't feel differently. The damage is entirely done to my future self. Only, now, my 17-year-old self's future is my 30-year-old self's present.

That's the reason I mention my diabetes. It's not to add the gravitas of illness to this narrative. It's because, as it turns out, all the doctors over the years who tried to convince me that I did, in fact, need to take my illness seriously weren't self-righteous morons. Or at least they weren't morons.

THE TESTS I take in the basement of DeerFields are mostly standard. I give blood. I have an ultrasound. I breathe into a tube. I take a series of complicated tests on a computer that maybe aren't complicated to other people, but they involve matching shapes and colours and remembering words. And I get a lot of answers wrong. To test my base fitness level, I'm fitted with a kind of Bane mask and I pedal as hard as I can on a stationary bicycle. Then I eat lunch. I'd mention the chef-prepared smoked pheasant, splash of corn chowder and elderberry salad, but that might be contrary to Dawn's request.

IN THE AFTERNOON, Dr. Knipping goes over the results with me. He's got white, close-shorn hair—in fact, the two other men who work at DeerFields have the same buzz cut, like monks devoted to healthcare. The two times I've met with him, he was wearing a shirt with a mandarin collar. When he smiles, it's the wide smile of a kid getting his picture taken at a party. You could imagine a world where he was called goofy. Only he isn't.

He tells me that one of the reasons he cares so much about aging is because he is so familiar with death. He worked as a coroner for five years. And he still works occasionally in a nearby ER. Somewhere in that crammed professional life, he found the time to be a psychologist, too. He's proud of the work he's done developing DeerFields, but it's the eagerness of a researcher, the joy of someone whose passion matches his work completely.

GOD BLESS DR. KNIPPING. Over the years, I've had doctors try a variety of tactics with me. They've appealed to my sense of independence. They've used guilt. They've become belligerent. I confounded all of them. It's like they aren't used to someone so fully resistant to the demands of his health. Or at least they aren't used to someone being so open about it.

But Dr. Knipping doesn't get dragged into that. He lets my test results speak for themselves. It starts off positive. My CardioAge—which measures how well my heart and arteries are doing—is 20. In terms of blood flow, I'm 10 years younger than my driver's license would tell you. My PulmoAge—that of my lungs—is 29, which is fine. A little better than average, but growing up Mormon will give you healthy lungs.

Then, my NeuroAge: I have the brain of a 54-year-old. "That just means you're wise," people tell me after I mention my results. But no. It means my cognitive function is that of a man on the far side of middle age. I have the kind of brain that will forget where the gas pedal is, who will drive slowly into a convenience store.

"Brain aging is a slow process," reads the DeerFields literature. "As early as your mid-twenties, certain aspects of your cognitive function begin to decline in a linear fashion. You don't notice until you tax the system...If that decline is steeper than the average person, you are more likely to have significant neurologic disease decades later..." My decline, at least according to this snapshot, is 24 years older than the average. At this rate, I'll be senile in, what, 10 years?

The rest of the results are just as bad, though somehow less depressing. My skin (not so much appearance, but elasticity) is 11 years older than me; my immune system is 52 years old, and I have the telomeres of a 49-year-old. And while my PhysioAge® Composite—a kind of comparison of my results against data aggregated from the results of 118 men and women over three years—is 30, it doesn't feel positive. Maybe everyone at 30 is broken.

There are other results, too, that only tangentially relate to my age, but increase my woe: my cholesterol is high, my blood sugars are too, and my testosterone is disturbingly low. Not only am I a man who is aging poorly, I'm also not much of a man.

Feeling wounded, I ask him why, if seemingly everything else in my body is falling apart sooner than it should, why my lungs and heart seem to be so fit. He tells me that the heart and lungs are sturdy. "So, they'll stay strong for a lot longer. It's really just that all the shit you put into your body—your energy drinks, your not taking care of your diabetes, your lack of exercise—they just haven't gotten to them yet."

"Your problem," Dr. Knipping tells me, eyes wide, "is that you've been too healthy." Then he talks about the regret men feel when they let their conditions—like my diabetes—take an eye or a limb. "They go two ways. It can wake them up, or they'll just say, 'Fuck it all,' and go down and down."

He swears more than you might expect. I suspect it's because I've cussed some, and like a good businessman, or psychologist (mostly likely both), he's subtly mirroring me. But the point is well taken. I still don't feel sick, or old, but I'm certainly not well. And I can ignore it like I always have or I can wake up. "Your desire to be alive today will be the same when you're 70 years old," the doctor says.

It would be easy to rationalize all this away, and not only because ignorance of scientific specifics can erode confidence in all medical professionals. But because aging is aging—it's as inevitable as winter—and whether you delay it or not, you'll still end up cold in the end. Fighting the aging process is, I tell myself, a result of a capitalist culture obsessed with youth, sex and consumption (and the first two are about the latter, anyway). I'll get old. So will you. And if I hadn't gone to DeerFields, I'd get old just the same.

But, of course, that's bullshit. Life isn't necessarily about quantity, it's about quality. And that's a cliché that you can post on your Facebook wall, superimposed over a picture of some beach somewhere, but it's also probably true. Age management is less about dying later, and more about enjoying to the fullest whatever life you've got.

So, what do I do, knowing that my life is getting shorter, faster?

I run.

It's not much. I didn't join DeerFields to avail myself of their fitness routine, personalized diet, proprietary supplements and hormonal therapy (which, I should say, I truly believe would help). I'm not an executive, and can't afford executive healthcare. I haven't even gone to an endocrinologist. I still don't have a family doctor. The difference is, now I'm actually entertaining the possibility of medical supervision. And while thinking about going to see a doctor makes no difference to my pancreas, I believe this is a step, however tentative, in the right direction.

But until then, there are things I do do. I eat fewer snacks. Less fried food. The same number of energy drinks, but I remember to take my insulin more. And I wake up early, put on my shoes, and no matter how bitterly cold it is, I run.

The disease I figured I'd deal with when I was older is actually making me older right now. So I run as a way of dealing with it. My thinking—and I realize full well that my thinking can be suspect, what with how old my brain is—is that if I can at least be a better diabetic, I'll have won a small victory over aging. It's what's killing me, after all: the sugar-sharpened blood that flows through my veins, damaging everything that blood touches: my eyes, my feet, my penis, my brain. If running will help take some of that sugar out of my blood, I'll be healthier. Everything will be better.

And, yes, I feel a little heroic about my improved fitness. And, yes, I've lost weight. But mostly, running is my way of shouting down all the feelings of despair and failure and anger I felt driving home from the age management clinic; the ones that wake me up and push me.

I also run as punishment. I'm punishing my body for not working. For aging too soon. For letting all that sugar float around in my blood instead of using it like normal bodies do. For making me acknowledge my mortality when I had planned on ignoring it until I was a grandfather. Fuck you, body. You were always going to fail me, but you're failing me too soon.

But punishment is also about correction. You punish your kids, not just to remind them of their wrongdoing, but so that their behaviour will change, improve. And I'm running to change my body. I'm correcting. I won't stop time, but I'll hopefully stop losing it.

Remember This

Kathleen Kennedy

When words become unclear, I shall focus with photographs.
When images become inadequate, I shall be content
with silence.
—Ansel Adams

THERE IS A photograph on my bookshelf of my mother as a young woman. It doesn't remind me of her at all, but for some reason fills me with nostalgia—for what exactly, I don't know. It is a colour photograph, but everything within the frame of the picture appears sepia in tone, giving the photograph a rich and warm glow, heavy on mood. She is seated and wears a dark, full skirt that is crammed full of taffeta. It fans out theatrically over gracefully posed legs. Luck has spilled the light so that the shadows accentuate all her best features. There is an elegance to her that seems to deny the possibility of a future life containing marriage, children, and a wardrobe of barn clothes. She could be a rising starlet or a gypsy queen. In her lap she cradles a small guitar. She *did* play the guitar, preferring three chord songs in the key of G, and I remember her stroking, rather than strumming the strings, which was soothing to listen to, if not technically impressive. I love this photograph. Overall it is artsy and posed, but the sixty years that have passed since it was taken have worked to almost fictionalize it. It might not quite be my mother in the picture, but there is a story here, and it is a long one; when I look at this picture, and I often do, I think it just might be the best story ever told.

A FEW YEARS ago I stood in a dimly lit gallery that was exhibiting the works of Yousuf Karsh. He drew a crowd. We shuffled sideways down the walls of black and white photographs, shoulder to shoulder, like guests before a receiving line. We were received handsomely. Most of the photographs were of people I recognized from other photographs—Albert Einstein, Humphrey Bogart, John F. Kennedy—but this time I was *meeting* them. I was seeing, not their likenesses, but their characters. I looked Pablo Picasso in the eye and thought, "Aha! I *knew* it!" I stood before Martha Graham and immediately realized the inadequacy of my fitness regime. When I think of Ernest Hemmingway or Winston Churchill it is Karsh's Hemmingway and Karsh's Churchill that I instantly conjure, for it seems that in these photographs the very essence of the man has been captured, making it impossible for me to separate subject from photo. It was considered a great privilege to be photographed by this polite and diminutive man, and I wonder what it would have been like to sit for him, knowing, as his subjects must have known, that he offered nothing short of immortality. Those who were photographed were said to have been "karshed."

ONE OF MY son's favourite pastimes is to take photographs of the members of our family. I prefer to watch. There is a stillness in him that I rarely get to see. As he loses himself in the task, he loses, too, his self-awareness, leaving himself open for scrutiny. So I watch. In my mind I propel him into adulthood the way only mothers do; I see him as the contemplative type, hope for him an artistic sensibility—a talent for seeing truth, and a genius for harnessing it. He looks through the camera and I imagine he is seeing what the shrewd and soulful eyes of Yousuf Karsh saw—that each subject possesses a rich and meaningful facial landscape. Later, I read to him some of Karsh's own words: *Within every man and woman a secret is hidden, and as a photographer it is my task to reveal it if I can. The revelation, if it comes at all, will come in a small fraction of a second with an unconscious gesture, a gleam of the eye, a brief lifting of the mask that all humans wear to conceal their innermost selves from the world.* I hope to inspire him and he blinks politely, but my husband rolls his eyes. "He's not going for *essence,*" he explains. "He's going for *goofy.*"

Of course he is right. A picture may be worth a thousand words, but there is room for play here—for instance, *which* words? Karsh, artist and professional, took photographs to document greatness, while kids with cameras eschew technique and go straight for the punch-line. When I see my son's photographs my vision of him as artist-in-the-making is derailed, for, being ten years old, he is only interested in the more gimmicky, distorting camera settings; no self-respecting boy would choose artistic merit over a good guffaw.

So, never mind Art; instead he turns us, one by one, into elongated, or inflated, or flattened parodies of ourselves. His pictures of me lean toward birdy-ness—my lips thin to a faint line in the shadow of a skeletal beak, my eyes slant into a hungry, carrion-stare. My husband fares no better— my son's photos of him seem somehow bent on proving a pivotal, genetic link to the Incredible Hulk. I suppose the camera must utilize the raw materials provided—my face leans toward thinness, my husband's to fleshiness, so my photos suggest hawkishness whereas my husband's suggest simply mass. None are flattering.

A while ago my son added a new series to his portfolio—pictures of my mother during a short hospital stay. Again, the link was obvious: my mother was an alien. A tiny face stared out from a disproportionately large head with empty, infinite eyes, her hair a white puffy nebula engulfing her head. She was utterly unrecognizable yet utterly recognizable.

When I was my son's age I wrote a biography of my grandmother for a school project. My teacher assured me that I would one day treasure it. I found it doubtful. I was pleased by my mark—a generous 95%, but my grandmother lived with my family so I couldn't imagine treasuring a grade-school project on someone so familiar and ordinary—and frankly, on someone so *old*. Of course he was right. I do treasure the project with its red underlining and loopy handwriting and it does, in fact, contain information about my grandmother's life that may otherwise have been lost. After forty years it carries weight and importance like a deed of land. I began to worry that my son's alien photos of my mother would take the place of a neatly penned, respectful biography. He too was documenting impressions of his grandmother, but would these images be the ones to remain with him, the ones to immortalize her? If Georgia O'Keefe had been "karshed," had my mother, then, been "punked?" I found myself reminding my son of the games he once played with his grandmother, the stories they read, the little cabin they built out of logs in the woods, like I could somehow reinforce family history by jarring loose some errant and elusive childhood memories.

MY MOTHER HAS Alzheimer's. I have had the course of this disease described to me many times. Most recently, I heard a nurse say that to have Alzheimer's is to "become more like oneself," implying that as a person's inhibitions break down their true nature shows through more readily. To be honest, I was barely listening to her. I had been living the disease through my mother for two years and was inured by definition. But later, I found myself thinking about the phrase. Becoming more like oneself is an odd idea. It seems to suggest that the remaining, un-afflicted population is, for whatever reason, *avoiding* the self. In some ways, it sounds very nice. To "become more like oneself" has a positive ring, like it might just be the final outpost on some enlightened path. This must be the "lifting of the mask" that Karsh referred to—the very truth that artists strive to reveal. It sounds sublime and deliberate—the ultimate goal, of course, must then be—not merely to become *more* like oneself, but to become *completely* oneself. Think of the accomplishment! Like Jedi knights we would live our lives having fulfilled the most mindful, personal quest. Many would argue that we can never really know another person—but *ourselves*? At the end of life, is there an ultimate sense of failure if we think we have not succeeded in becoming ourselves in the most complete way?

This is not, however, the "becoming" that is experienced by those with dementia. Rarely is it positive or enlightening. Becoming more like oneself in this respect presents, unfortunately, a sadder image. The familiar characteristics, the whims and fancies, the quirky habits—the things that make us *us*—become grossly exaggerated: a love of ice cream, an affection for cats, a deep-rooted thriftiness, an inappetence for chit-chat, become *more,* turning into an insatiable craving for sweets, a smothering, incessant neediness, a kaleidoscope of paranoia, and a vocalized contempt, until one resembles, not so much one's former self, but some grossly-proportioned caricature of the former self. It is not a fulfillment, but a reduction.

For the first two years after my mother's diagnosis my sister and I, and our families, cared for my mother full-time. We split shifts—juggling families, work, outside obligations to make sure there was always someone with her when she was climbing out her bedroom window with her cat, taking midnight walks in the neighbour's field, or (when the matches were hidden) lighting the woodstove with newspapers first set ablaze in the toaster. We took a passive approach to care-giving; we shook the cat kibble from our shoes, emptied the sherry glasses brimming with balsamic vinegar, mopped up the WD-40 used for furniture polish, retrieved clothing from the branches of trees, and stomped out small household fires. She had always been a strong, independent, and resourceful person so the idea of imposing restrictions on her was difficult. For the most part we didn't interfere with her schedule of activities, however peculiar; instead we skewed our way of looking at things—climbing out the window wasn't so bad when you lived in a bungalow, getting lost in the woods can be fun, as long as your grandkids have been silently stalking you between the trees waiting to bring you home. The rest became the stuff of our daily lives: we removed tubs of ice cream from the dishwasher, separated cat kibble from the cinnamon sticks, and fished slices of salami out of the teapot. We kept the tone light, sharing with our friends the names we had coined for our new kitchen staples: Rinse-Cycle Ice Cream, Cinnamon Crunchies, Salami Tea. We watched her phase through different and inexplicable stages of the disease: for several months she adopted the lifestyle of a cat, endlessly sleeping, curled on a cushion in the sun. A more manic version weeded the lawn from dawn to dusk. We let her cycle through each phase in her own time; we took her drinks and sunhats and hoped the neighbours wouldn't judge us too harshly. When we did intervene with ideas about day programs and support services we were met with stubborn refusal. Was this the right approach? There is no way to tell. We aimed for the least disruptive path and did our best. When new problems arose we dealt with them furtively: we installed alarms on the doors, we screwed her windows shut, we hired someone to "walk the dogs" to give us a break for two hours a day.

Eventually social services, tiring from the effort of hiding their incredulity at our latest blunders (the time, for instance, when I found the "dog-walker" lying in the ditch with a broken shoulder, while mom, dressed in pyjamas and high-heels, lay prostrate beside her holding on to the two dogs who were still struggling to chase the squirrel that brought this scene about) suggested that Mom's condition warranted a more professional approach (we received full marks for the creative approach). Within three months we were dealing with the move to a nursing home. My mom was "more than ready" everyone insisted. They were right. She was *safe*, they assured us. But they were wrong, too. There were no cats to keep her company and no more weeds to pull; there was nothing meaningful or useful for her to do. But she was *safe*, they reminded us.

So, when Mom began to ask why she couldn't stay at home we played the Safety card with confidence. We reminded her about the time she was lost for eighteen hours and was only found due to the efforts of neighbours, police, K-9 units, helicopters and infrared technology. We told her we couldn't risk her getting lost and not being found. *Why not?* she said. *Is that so bad?*

I know she meant it. So now I am bothered by the image of her curled peacefully against the trunk of a tree deep in the forest she loved, played against the image of a slow, mindless, *safe* deterioration into nothingness. Safety, she would say, is for sissies.

One night she is there in my dreams. She looks confused. "Tell me how this is supposed to work," she says to me.

THERE IS A tree in our woods that has been dead longer than I can remember—certainly it was already dead when I was a child. Once it was a huge and majestic maple, but time, wildlife, and battalions of insects have worn the trunk into a pillar of ridges and blackened cavities. It now stands a mere fifteen feet tall—short as far as trees go, but still tall enough to look up to and still too large for me to wrap my arms around. It has been dead for decades, yet still it has the stately presence of a friendly forest giant. Years ago, long before forgetfulness began to claim my mother's life, she placed one palm against the trunk and told my daughter that she was having a contest with the tree to see who would better stand the test of time. My daughter was no more than five or six at the time, but she remembers her grandmother's words and I know she recalls them every time she walks past the tree in the woods. As I do. There is something soothing about that tree—its decay is noticeable, yet imperceptible. There is such peace—a complete absence of struggle; there is no bewilderment about the process. It is not grief, but wonder I feel over this tree's demise—wonder that something should know not just when, but *how* to quit.

IT IS AN "awful place" she tells my sister and me. For the most part, we agree. She is in a locked ward that screams incarceration. We visit, loaded with chocolates or donuts hoping to distract her from her one great purpose—escape. We cannot appeal to her reason so we appeal to her sweet tooth. "Try to make some friends," we say and introduce her to Art, who, as if we had mispronounced his name, corrects us patiently by saying, "It's Art *the Fart.*" When we take our leave of him Mom says, almost flirtatiously, "See you later, then," but Art only laughs and says, "Oh, I won't be here."

We are talking about travel. My sister asks, "If you could be anywhere in the world right now, where would you be?" Even the question makes her tired. "I don't really have any ambition to go anywhere," she says. I glance at the window whose hardware has recently been removed. Only yesterday she had been caught with one leg through the six inch opening the window allowed. Her moods and thoughts slide in and out. Like Lear she is capable of acting outraged and conciliatory in a single, turbulent moment. Her weariness is relaxing for us, but we know better than to confuse it with contentment.

After the first six weeks my sister and I meet with the nursing home staff for our first "resident care meeting." No longer allowed to drift through her days, Mom now has a schedule for eating, and sleeping, and bathing, and dressing, and exercise. We discuss her nutrition plan, her medications, her physiotherapy, her mood, her bowel activity, her interaction with the other residents and staff. She is no longer allowed to sit with Art the Fart at meal times we are told. They are worried that between the two of them they will succeed in cooking up a viable escape plan. *Let them plot* we want to say, but we don't—we defer to their expertise in such matters. I surprise myself by discovering that I am actually rooting for them; in my mind they are like POWs—*Hogan's Heroes*-style—happy-go-lucky pranksters whose duty, first and foremost, is to encourage each other, at all costs, to escape. I can't begrudge them the fun of hatching a grand escape plan and the ultimate triumph of beating the system. I look around the table at the nurses, nutritionists, and administrators and wonder if they know I am seeing them as the enemy. I tune back into the meeting in time to receive the final assessment: Mom was "not adjusting well."

Not adjusting well? At first I wonder if they are reading from the wrong file—the file of a resident with physical disabilities perhaps. I look at my sister and see she is just as confused. Had Mom not been admitted to the nursing home *because* she was no longer capable of adjusting? If she was expected to *adjust* was she then also expected to *get better?*

IN THE TIME she has been there her hair has grown into a wild, fluffy fleece around her face; it diminishes her features, reminding me again of those distorted photographs my son took a year ago. I remember the way he had concentrated to take those pictures—I felt I had really *seen* him; I had glimpsed such quiet intelligence beneath the mask of boyish behaviour. When I look at my mother now I am struck by the absolute absence of concentration, and I know I will never really see her again. It is as if her mask has been lifted, only too late. Her innermost self is gone, yet here she is. We sit on her bed and eat oatmeal cookies and she gazes out the window to guess at the season. The icicles that stab down from the roof provide no clues. "Is it June already?" I feel guilty when I leave, thinking we could have kept her home longer. Is not knowing the month reasonable grounds for eviction? Has inconvenience become so intolerable to us that we can't bother ourselves to retrieve the cutlery from the flower bed now and then? In a way this fuzzy-haired, crazy-lady look helps to convince me of the need for institutional care, helps explain this wooly disease. The other part of me (the part that doesn't need convincing because it remembers the flaming tea towels in the oven) wonders why we are so inept that we can't even manage to arrange a hair appointment. She doesn't need to look like a madwoman. We shouldn't need to be convinced.

All her adult life my mother has cut her own hair. She cut it short and she cut it quickly. There was no real artistry involved (the haircuts she gave my sister and me as children were disastrous), but she had thick, forgiving hair and a slight build, so that she always managed to pull off a wavy, not-quite stylish, Jackie Kennedy look. One day I bark out some lines from her beloved Wodehouse, *Why don't you get a haircut? You look like a chrysanthemum!* But she doesn't remember the joke and just waves the idea aside. "I'll just do it myself," she says. *With scissors?* I imagine the nurses' faces. A week earlier she had whacked a nurse in the shin with her cane for not letting her walk the ten kilometres home. I book the appointment.

Another six weeks passes and we are still hoping for adjustment. Five minutes after lunch she cannot remember having eaten, but she recites the ancient Greek alphabet without pause. I arrive one day and she is singing "Somewhere Over the Rainbow." She sings it *a tempo*, flawlessly and in entirety. She inquires about her own mother who has been dead for twenty years. She still asks to come home, although with slightly less conviction because she can't remember where home is. She has become less agitated and more philosophical lately. "It's not a bad life," she tells me. "I just don't understand it."

Yet every visit we unpack her belongings which are

stuffed into the tied arms and legs of her pajamas and tossed in the bottom of her wardrobe-like effigies awaiting public humiliation. As we leave we ask her if she would like to watch a DVD. Many have gone missing, the selection is limited. She picks up *Cover Girl.* "I can always watch Rita Hayworth," she says, but it isn't said as a concession like *we can always eat leftovers*, rather, she means it literally—she can *always* watch Rita Hayworth. We say goodbye and tell her our girls will be by to visit after school. She doesn't *always* remember her grandchildren.

She believes now, most days, that she works at the nursing home, which she thinks is a library. But now, she tells us, she has had enough. She has written at least four letters of resignation to the nursing staff, explaining that she can no longer manage the job and will be returning home. Her notes are apologetic, yet decisive. The latest one is short and to the point, it reads like the teasing, closing lines of a children's story. TO WHOM IT MAY CONCERN: I HAVE GONE HOME. WHO KNOWS WHAT NEXT! LOVE ELEANOR P.S. CALL ME IF YOU NEED ME. I feel a surge of joy to see that it is not her sense of adventure that has been lost, only her sense of direction.

So I read out loud to her. She lies on her bed, enjoying the rare blanket of sun that pours through the February window. I am reading *Alice in Wonderland*. She remembers it more clearly than I do. *I can't explain* myself, *I'm afraid sir,' said Alice, 'because I am* not *myself, you see.* She remembers not only the words, but can chuckle at both the predicament and the sentiment. Surely these are subtleties that only a beautifully working mind can comprehend, yet, like Alice, she cannot begin to explain herself, for the self is lost. What is left in its stead is an ever-changing landscape of memories. Some days, things are black and white and filled

with light—you might discover a shrewd insight for literature, or a rekindled infatuation for movie stars of old. It is a
place to find a favourite song, or an ancient alphabet. Other
days the landscape blurs into an unfocussed expanse, a place
of otherwordly, underdeveloped images that we can't begin
to decipher or navigate our way through. Over time the
light fades and the landscape becomes less habitable. For a
while a haircut can fool the family, but not for long. Without memories we don't know who we are and do not recognize those who lack them. They interpret the self, they steer
the "unconscious gestures," fuel the "gleam of the eye" that
Karsh aimed to capture in his brilliant photographs.

It is now a familiar walk down the hall to Mom's room.
The other residents line the wall in their chairs and wheel-
chairs. The postures vary only slightly. Some greet us, most
do not. This, too, is a portrait gallery of sorts, but does not
draw the crowds. There is resistance as you walk, the memories here are knee-deep. The shedding is mostly soundless,
the landscape empties. You watch, but try to redirect your
thoughts to the kinder, more dignified decay of a forest tree.
You can only watch—your mother, or father, your husband,
or wife as they turn into some unrecognizable/recognizable
caricature of the person they once were. And then one day
you realize, so very cruelly, that they resemble nothing so
much as a ten-year-old-boy's idea of a joke.

Armed and Dangerous

JOHN LORINC

WHEN POLITICAL SCIENTIST Adam Molnar was working on his doctoral thesis at the University of Victoria a few years ago, he unearthed an unnerving development among Canadian police departments. In the early 2000s, an unnamed source told him, the Vancouver Police Department established what it calls a military liaison unit, or MLU. This elite team coordinated the Canadian Forces troops assigned to the 2010 Winter Olympics, an event with a $1 billion security budget.

Through in-depth, off-the-record interviews with VPD insiders, as well as access-to-information requests, Molnar determined that in the run-up to the games a senior police officer with military experience identified a need for "interoperability" between the department and the Canadian Forces. The officer's goal: create clear lines of communication, demarcate jurisdictions, and address chain-of-command issues.

The senior officer pitched the idea to the VPD chief at the time, Jamie Graham, who had grown up on army bases and approved of the concept. The VPD then assigned more than two dozen police officers to a new unit—all of them specially trained to respond to such crisis events as major earthquakes—along with two dozen or more Canadian troops. "It was a perfectly reasonable justification," Molnar told me.

I contacted Molnar, who now teaches at Deakin University in Melbourne, Australia, late one afternoon through Twitter. The young researcher responded almost immediately. Neither the VPD nor the Canadian Forces, he explained, had disclosed information about their joint operations. There hadn't been public oversight of the unit's activities, either. The aura of secrecy, he said, should make everyone "sit up straight and ask more questions."

Ask more questions is just what Molnar has done: as he peeled the onion, he discovered that Vancouver's MLU had quietly expanded beyond its original mandate. In fact, the senior officer who set it up had pitched the idea to other police services, including those in Calgary, Victoria, and some cities in Atlantic Canada. (A spokesperson for the Toronto Police Service, Canada's largest municipal force, said its 5,500-officer force does not include an MLU.) More troubling, Molnar learned, those assigned to the Vancouver MLU travel regularly, along with other Canadian cops, to a base in Yakima, Washington, where they work alongside members of the US National Guard on urban law enforcement techniques. In effect, the police officers are receiving military instruction. Is this how we want to train those who will come back to patrol the streets of our cities?

WE LIVE IN a world of mission creep, a world where the lines that once separated local policing and national security have become profoundly entangled. On one level, that blurring is intentional—a rational response to the globalization of organized crime, terrorism, and borderless online activities like identity theft and child pornography. On another level, it's not always intentional. Insular municipal police departments have inadvertently found themselves with the tools of war, and are using them to guarantee domestic tranquility. Perhaps nothing demonstrates this dynamic more vividly than what happened this past August in Ferguson, Missouri.

As images of a two-week military-style siege went viral—following the police-shooting death of Michael Brown, an unarmed black teenager, in the St. Louis suburb—people around the world asked, How did all that equipment end up in the hands of a suburban enforcement agency? How does such a small agency come to look and act like an expeditionary force?

It happens when the US Defense Department, through a program established in the early 1990s and known only as 1033, off-loads more than $5 billion worth of gear to 8,000 state and local police forces, along with a handful of school districts. Ferguson, a city of 21,000 people, isn't exactly a forward operating base in Afghanistan. Yet its cops apparently keep armoured vehicles, night-vision goggles, assault rifles, and assorted battle gear on hand, just in case things get ugly.

Questions about whether there was a Canadian version of 1033 came hard on the heels of Ferguson. The short answer: it exists, but on a much smaller scale. The Directorate Disposal, Sales, Artefacts and Loans, a division of the Department of National Defence, oversees transfers, subject to various regulations of the Treasury Board. DND spokesperson Ashley Lemire told me that municipal or provincial police services can request surplus *matériel* through the solicitor general's office. The defence minister's staff then reviews those requests on a "case-by-case basis."

As the protests unfolded in Missouri, Canadian media reports itemized the gear cops here had amassed. Postmedia, for example, reported that the Canadian Forces had transferred night-vision goggles, webbing, and field equipment to the RCMP over the years, while police forces in Edmonton, Windsor, Ontario, and New Glasgow, Nova Scotia, had received "de-armed" armoured fighting vehicles. Saskatoon police used their own AFV in a recent standoff, and released aerial footage of the incident to underscore how the vehicle keeps cops and civilians safe.

Other cities, including Ottawa, have purchased military vehicles and other surplus gear. According to the *Vancouver Sun*, the VPD bought a $270,000 Lenco BearCat armoured rescue vehicle in 2007, with fundraising by the police association covering the bulk of the cost. A few years later, York Region, the sprawling municipality of a million people north of Toronto, acquired a $340,000 Quebec-made "rolling fortress," the *Globe and Mail* revealed. In Montreal and Quebec City, cops have taken to wearing camouflage pants, a practice that has raised eyebrows. The CBC reported last year that Windsor police bought fifteen high-powered carbine rifles to replace older and less accurate shotguns—a move that twenty other police services in Ontario had already made.

While Windsor cops are receiving training with their new rifles, they haven't yet field-tested their de-armoured military vehicle, a Cougar the Canadian Forces donated earlier this year. In September, emergency responders in the city rushed to a dramatic standoff in a working-class neighbourhood, with a gunman holed up in an apartment. More than fifty cops, including heavily armed members of the local SWAT team, cordoned off the area. They were supported by command-unit buses and police cruisers; the department intends to use the Cougar only when an active shooter is on the loose.

Overall, Canadian cops aren't as heavily armed as their American counterparts. And experts emphasize that the militarization that does exist—motivated by counter-terrorism efforts, proactive intelligence gathering, and stepped-up emergency preparedness—falls far short of the sort of thing we saw in Ferguson.

"I don't see direct parallels between Canada and the US," Neil Boyd, a criminologist at Simon Fraser University in Burnaby, British Columbia, told me. If anything, he has observed a trend toward de-escalation. But the growing reliance on weaponry in local law enforcement "is worrying on one level, because we think of militarization as armed conflict between states," Boyd said. "As a society, that's not consistent with the police model of keeping the peace. The question we have to ask is, Are the police more inclined to take an us-and-them approach, or are they simply acquiring more technology?"

The post-Ferguson spotlight on the overt militarization of policing has focussed on the most tangible evidence—the proliferation of weaponry and combat gear that most people encounter only in Hollywood blockbusters and shoot-'em-up video games. Yet the quiet expansion of military liaison units underscores another, more pernicious phenomenon: the subtle and not-so-subtle tactics geared toward occupation, control, and surveillance. This is where the Canadian story becomes much less comforting.

THE SLIPPERY SLOPE of "security thinking" is all too familiar—just think of the cameras aimed at public spaces, massive electronic eavesdropping campaigns carried out by the Communications Security Establishment Canada and the National Security Agency, or workplaces dutifully defended against intruders and maniacs by swipe-card entry systems. In the wake of Ferguson, I contacted Veronica Kitchen, a security expert at the University of Waterloo in Ontario. She often asks her students to consider the full-body scanners that now greet passengers at major airports (baggage and supplies find their way onto planes with far less scrutiny). They don't think twice about measures that "were all exceptions at one point." That's the truly disturbing detail, she told me: society has come to accept such searches, video surveillance, and the presence of armed transit cops without questioning whether these intrusions actually make us safer, or merely more wary.

I emailed the VPD and asked about its military liaison unit of thirty officers. Spokesperson Randy Fincham acknowledged it had been involved in joint "military/civil" training programs, but declined to offer much more in the way of specifics. For Molnar—who maintains that there is no "meaningful public disclosure and consultation" about such training exercises, especially those taking place outside Canada—the VPD's official position was inadequate. "The joint nature of the program shows that the MLU is not just a small unit," he wrote in an email after I forwarded him the VPD's statement. "Its members are often recruited on the basis of their previous experience in military situations, arguably not a valuable credential to serve and protect Vancouver's communities and neighbourhoods."

The VPD program is but one example of a largely invisible expansion of highly coordinated militaristic tactics involving municipal police services and other agencies. Since 9/11, according to government documents obtained by criminologists Jeffrey Monaghan and Kevin Walby, nuclear facilities in Ontario have ramped up their security operations, establishing paramilitary-style teams to defend plant perimeters. In the event of a security breach, these teams are trained to work closely with local and provincial police forces; Ontario Power Generation also hires local cops and private guards to staff off-site command posts and participate in joint training drills.

In recent years, to cite a more urban example, police in low-income Toronto neighbourhoods have employed the Toronto Anti-Violence Intervention Strategy to curb turf wars between rival gangs. Following a major bust, large teams of officers virtually blanket communities, ostensibly to prevent more violence and to reassure residents. (These so-called guns-and-gangs investigations frequently involve investigators from the TPS, the Ontario Provincial Police, the RCMP, and the Canadian Border Services Agency, as well as the FBI and the Bureau of Alcohol, Tobacco, Firearms and Explosives.) John Sewell, a former Toronto mayor and long-time police watchdog, told me that 24-7 patrols are a waste of resources and that the net effect of random ID checks heightens the sense of insecurity—and disproportionally targets young black males. "The police literally try to go in and occupy a community," he said. "They are supposed to be part of the community, not occupying it. That's a military thing to do."

THE PRE-EMPTIVE MINDSET of the urban-military security cordon could not be more removed from the democratic principles that informed the birth of domestic policing. In the early 1830s, British prime minister Sir Robert Peel instituted the first modern municipal police service, dispatching peace officers—"bobbies" or "peelers"—across London to replace a patchwork of private runners and guards.

Peel famously believed that the police are the community and that the community is the police, and his philosophy influenced law enforcement in both Canada and the

US. Under the Insurrection Act of 1807 and the Posse Co-
mitatus Act—a Reconstruction policy passed in 1878 and
kept in place until 1981—American soldiers were not allowed to touch domestic law enforcement. That principle
has been dying the death of a thousand tough-on-crime
bills since the Reagan administration. In fact, US law enforcement had become increasingly militaristic since the
1960s, thanks to the backlash against the civil rights movement and the advent of SWAT teams. Over the last three
decades, the war on drugs, the war on illegal aliens, the war
on terror, the war on international money laundering, and
countless other rhetorical battles have changed the very nature of domestic law enforcement.

In 2001, US international relations experts Peter An-
dreas and Richard Price noted that Cold War surveillance
technologies had been adapted for drug- and border-con-
trol operations, as well as municipal policing, under the en-
couragement of federal lawmakers and military officials.
Along the way, police tactics had become increasingly militaristic. Thirteen years later, the situation has only gotten
more pronounced.

Consider the seemingly indispensable SWAT team. In
The Rise of the Warrior Cop, Radley Balko, a *Washington
Post* crime reporter, explains how it didn't even exist until
a thirty-nine-year-old Los Angeles police inspector infor-
mally consulted a Marine unit and effectively changed "the
face, the mind-set, and the culture of US policing" forever.

Fifty years ago, for six days in August 1965, racially
charged violence and unrest swept through Watts, a densely
populated LA neighbourhood. In response, the police chief
charged Inspector Daryl Gates with running a new tactical
operations unit, to combat what was seen as a virulent form
of racial urban warfare. Gates recruited skilled marksmen

and set up several military-style squads, and named his creation Special Weapons and Tactics. He went on to investigate the Manson Family murders and the Hillside Strangler, before becoming chief in 1978 and resigning in the wake of the 1992 Rodney King riots. But as the father of the SWAT team, his real legacy was to devise an aggressive response approach that radically undermined Peel's foundational principles.

As I thought about how the proliferation of guns, mass shootings, and cop killings have propelled SWAT teams and the use of formidable weaponry, I asked Greg Bennett, a security consultant and retired lieutenant with the Middlesex Sheriff's Department in New Jersey, about the spread of military thinking. He pointed to a particularly violent bank robbery that occurred in LA a decade ago: thieves shot several officers and civilians before the SWAT team arrived. That incident, he said, "sent out shock waves internationally" and triggered a push for better body armour, military-grade assault weapons, and AFVs that many people are only now noticing. The outlays can be significant, he acknowledged, but "the public will get behind you if they are afraid of what can happen."

The 2013 Boston Marathon bombing, which killed four people and injured hundreds of others, fostered a similar response among police departments tasked with securing mass public events. Before the 2014 race, according to local news affiliates, Boston's bomb squad acquired state-of-the-art portable robots designed to remotely defuse or detonate explosives. Some 3,500 officers, twice the 2013 contingent, were on hand, and the heightened security measures included bomb-sniffing dogs, additional cameras, and restrictions on bags that spectators and participants could bring to the event. New York, Chicago, and Philadelphia also bolstered security provisions for their marathons. New York's organizers, in fact, doubled their security budget to $1 million and hired a private security firm to do a full review of its safety policies.

There are also seemingly less obvious responses, such as tourniquets. Since the 2013 bombings, according to *USA Today*, many police forces have equipped their officers with the simple devices. The move may be a cost-effective response to tragedy, but it nonetheless reflects a change in mindset, one that anticipates the domestic sphere being transformed into a field hospital.

GovSec, a massive expo for homeland security equipment and services in Washington, DC, helps to disseminate new technologies and tactics. As the strong attendance at this year's show suggests, the industry is enormous and growing quickly. According to Homeland Security Research—a DC-based market research firm whose clients include the US Congress, NATO, and the Government of Canada—the global homeland security and public safety markets are dominated by American companies, and will balloon from $305 billion in 2011 to $546 billion in 2022. The tally includes billions spent globally on so-called safe cities projects.

Each year, the trade show attracts police from around the world, and features panel discussions and training seminars. At the same time, equipment suppliers ply their wares to a captive and sympathetic audience. Not surprisingly, there's nothing subtle about their pitches: many fill their promotional materials with images that recall in-the-trenches screen grabs from violent video games.

Greg Bennett is a member of the GovSec advisory board and knows first-hand how militarized law enforcement tactics spread around the world. He told me that many US police departments are looking for equipment that will better protect front-line officers, who must do their jobs in a society awash with military-grade weapons: "We've had a lot of issues in recent years with officers being outgunned." But his tone was more matter of fact when he mentioned international agencies and customers who eagerly invest in security equipment meant to "harden"—a military term—facilities from oil refineries to elementary schools against armed intruders. As he put it, "Have you heard about Columbine?"

LIKE MANY CANADIAN cops, Robert Chrismas, a Winnipeg staff sergeant who recently wrote *Canadian Policing in the 21st Century*, is keenly aware of the threats facing American law enforcement. Stories about downed officers are so common on US police blogs that he had to stop following them: they're too depressing. The tales about officer safety prompted Chrismas' own department to upgrade its SWAT team from part-time to full-time, and the unit is now deployed for high-risk takedowns. "It's the safest way to deal with these situations," Chrismas explains. He tellingly describes his world as a "battleground." Other police agencies have put forward similar explanations to justify the purchase of everything from armoured vehicles to tasers.

Those who follow Canadian crime statistics point out that the risk levels are at historical lows. Indeed, violent crime has fallen so dramatically in recent years that the Fraser Institute came out with a study earlier this fall calling for reductions in police staffing levels. Given the trends, John Sewell believes cities should be thinking about eliminating some firearms and other so-called less lethal weapons, including tasers, as a way of rebuilding the social connections between law enforcement and the public. "It's important to pull back from that approach," the former mayor said.

That suggestion, of course, is a non-starter in today's tough-on-crime political environment. Instead of de-escalating, Canada seems to be expanding a form of security-oriented policing, influenced by such events as the Vancouver Winter Olympics, the 2010 G20 Toronto summit, and next summer's Pan Am and Parapan American Games in Toronto.

Waterloo University's Veronica Kitchen, who is also a fellow at the Balsillie School of International Affairs, observes that mega-events funnel military tactics and equipment into the bloodstream of Canadian law enforcement agencies. And then there's the matter of private-security armies that augment the overall policing plan, without accountability or public oversight. Organizers of both the Olympics and the G20, for example, relied heavily on Contemporary Security Canada—a subsidiary of a US firm that bills itself as "the leader in crowd management"—to supply hundreds of private guards to work alongside police, riot squads, and other public agencies in a highly integrated, military-style operation. As it happens, that same company has won a contract for the Pan Am Games. The total security cost is estimated at $239 million, and will likely grow by next summer.

Besides the privatization of security, mass events result in large one-time equipment purchases, which have unforeseeable uses. "It's often at these events where police forces can argue they need extra security equipment," Kitchen told me. In a study published this year in *International Political Sociology*, she and Wilfrid Laurier University professor Kim Rygiel illustrated how the security thinking that characterizes a special event can be integrated into normal policing—a dynamic that's evocative of the dramatic expansion of the SWAT teams. Kitchen and Rygiel cite, by way of example, the seventy-one CCTV cameras that the Toronto Police Service installed before the G20, at a cost of more than $700,000. After world leaders left town, the department decided to keep fifty-two of them, to be deployed around major downtown intersections, despite a dearth of evidence that such equipment deters criminals in public spaces. As Kitchen said, "There isn't a terrorist on every corner."

The most questionable equipment legacy of the G20, however, was the purchase of several sound cannons, which can induce vomiting and can even make human bones vibrate. The cannons, Kitchen and Rygiel point out, were originally developed by the US military to fight Somali pirates and Iraqi insurgents, but found their way to the 2009 Pittsburgh G20 summit. Amid controversy over the decision to keep the sonic weapons, TPS chief Bill Blair insisted that they'll only be used by the marine unit and in emergency situations when other communications systems fail. Nonetheless, "function creep" is a real concern. As Kitchen put it to me: if a tool is there, it's likely to get used—and not necessarily for the stated purpose. "These decisions happen under the radar," she said. Moreover, there's no guarantee that Blair's order won't be altered by a tough-minded successor.

Adam Molnar, the Canadian political scientist, is worried about similar function creep with drone use. Police departments in a growing number of US cities have already added unmanned aerial vehicles to their arsenal of equipment.

At the moment, drone use in Canadian airspace, by any entity other than the military, is strictly regulated by Transport Canada, which is primarily concerned with aviation safety rather than crime prevention. While provincial police forces have flown them over traffic accidents and in search-and-rescue missions, they remain off-limits for municipal police services. As the federal privacy commissioner noted in a 2013 discussion paper on the topic, "Law enforcement represents the greatest potential users of small drones domestically because they offer a simple and cost effective alternative to airborne law enforcement activities." Unsurprisingly, the report flagged privacy and intrusive stealth surveillance as obvious concerns.

Should Canadians be worried about military drones being dispatched to support domestic criminal investigations? Molnar thinks it's a valid concern, and warns that military liaison units could facilitate unauthorized drone surveillance. "When you look at the way information sharing is occurring between the military and the police, this creates the opportunity for the MLU to become the conduit between the police and Canadian Forces drones. The full implications have yet to be revealed."

THE EVENTS OF Ferguson, though shocking visually, should not have come as a surprise. For years, the transfer of equipment from the military to police forces has not only continued apace, it has been encouraged and lauded by local and national authorities. Law enforcement officials have been reaping the benefits of the technology that has flowed out of the military-industrial complex for decades. And as security consultant Greg Bennett reminded me, the 2008 financial crisis accelerated the transfer, with cash-strapped police departments eyeing the windfall of deeply discounted *matériel* left over from the Iraq war.

Here, in Canada, we may feel smug about our low crime rates and the fact that our police forces don't, for the most part, dress and act like RoboCops. Yet Molnar, who is now researching the social and privacy implications of domestic drone use, maintains that Canadian officers are hardly immune from the influence of military techniques and the pervasive security thinking that permeates virtually every sphere of society—from private homes to schools, offices, and public spaces. More troubling is the fact that our civilian oversight bodies have failed to put a check on these instances of mission creep, even when there's no defensible reason for keeping the information about the activities of police operations, such as military liaison units, away from the public.

In some ways, Ferguson, for all its awfulness, may be more straightforward to counter, because the world got to see, once and for all, how a modest American police department sought to deploy its arms on the front lines of an imagined race war. So far in Canada, the militarization of policing is more about the practices than the stuff. Our cops have all the body armour. They just wear it on the inside.

Crime and Punishment

Sinéad Mulhern

RIGHT BEFORE WE met for the first time, Ava[1] sends a text. "I got here early." She includes a description: the blonde woman wearing black. My bike bumps along Toronto's Dundas Street bringing me closer to the café where we've agreed to meet. It's an airy café, fairly full. Neatly framed artwork has been arranged, carefully decorating its walls. On this late October 2013 evening, it's about a half hour until sunset. Nearly golden light streams in and coffee cups clink on saucers as I walk down the row of tables looking for Ava. A blonde woman sits alone. I see her from the back first. She's wearing black. It's her.

We introduce ourselves politely. When Ava smiles the corners of her eyes crinkle a little. Her blonde hair falls in soft waves just past her shoulders. She wears a freshly scented fragrance and subtle makeup. At 41, she wouldn't look out of place lecturing behind a university podium, dashing down Bay Street in the morning, or picking a child up from school. Ava starts our conversation with, "I like your nail polish," and in the same girlish raspy voice she says, "My story is complicated." For the past several years, Ava has been a prisoner inside Grand Valley Institute, a Kitchener,

---

[1] *name changed to protect privacy*

Ont.-based federal institute for women. She began serving her sentence in 2007, and was released on early parole in 2008; by 2009, she'd re-offended and was back in prison. In May 2013 she was released on parole again, a series of drug trafficking and fraud charges behind her—or at least starting to be.

While at Grand Valley, Ava earned a degree from Laurentian University. She is now going to college, planning a career helping women who have been abused. On the surface, it all sounds good, but as Ava has told me, her story is complicated. While she's believes she held privileges in prison—being white-skinned and educated—in many ways, she also thrived *despite* the criminal justice system. She's a rare success story born from a poorly-run prison, where the system is anything but conducive to rebuilding women's lives—even though, as a rethink of the punitive model, it was designed to do exactly that. In a very real sense, she is one of the lucky unlucky ones.

Ava tells me she recently moved out of the halfway house, where, as part of her parole, she was mandated to live from May until October. The server brings her a mug of chai tea and almond milk as I do the math: This is her fifth day of complete independence in years. Ava looks up at the server. "Can I have two sugars, too?"

A Canadian woman with a sentence of two years or more serves her time in federal prison. *Orange is the New Black* may have viewers captivated by the idea of what serving time is like but there's more going on between scenes—in the Canadian system and at Grand Valley in particular. Between March 2010–March 2012, the population of federally sentenced women topped 600 for the first time, representing a 21 percent increase in just two years. Inside the grey of Grand Valley, women live packed like maraschino cherries in a jar. There, the population is about 180, or three times what the institution was originally designed to accommodate. Gymnasiums, visiting units, and the interview room of the maximum security unit have become makeshift cells. The max unit, where high-security offenders stay, now has two beds in cells that were only designed to hold one.

On top of this, Canada's prison ombudsperson, Howard Sapers, is concerned about violence in Canada's women's institutions. Inmate fights, use-of-force interventions, self-harm, and charges during prison stays and are all trending in the wrong direction. About 69 percent of women offenders also needed mental-health treatment in 2010–2011. Most of the women, 85 percent, have physical abuse in their past and 68 percent have been sexually abused. Family visits are rare—there are only five female-only prisons in Canada (plus a healing lodge) and many incarcerated women have been transported great distances. Sometimes prisoners' families are even blocked from getting inside.

Grand Valley wasn't supposed to be like this. Opened in 1997, the prison was designed to be an alternative to the Kingston Prison for Women's (P4W) rigid and inhospitable environment. Until its closure in 2000, the Kingston prison housed every woman convicted of a federal offence in the country, no matter which corner of Canada she came from. During its 66 years, the prison was under constant scrutiny. From its opening until 1993, it faced 13 investigations commissioned by the government, many of which suggested the prison be shut down. Lack of programming, education, and therapy combined with distance from family lead to inmate despair, depression, claustrophobia, self-harming, and suicide. Between 1977–1991, at least 12 women committed suicide while incarcerated.

In response, the Task Force on Federally Sentenced Women, including members of the government and advocacy groups such as the Elizabeth Fry Society and the Native Women's Association of Canada, released a report called "Creating Choices" in April 1990. It outlined areas that needed to be improved for women serving their sentences. After its release, it was decided the Kingston Prison for Women was unfit and would close (at least in theory) in 1994. Then, in the year it was supposed to have closed, a video surfaced, showing an April incident in which male guards brought eight inmates out of their cells for strip searches; they cavity searched seven of the eight the following day. At one point, inmates were also left in empty cells wearing nothing but paper gowns, and in restraints and leg irons. It was a pivotal point in garnering media attention—and even more criticism. It took from 1990–2000 for every single woman to be moved out of the prison and then it finally shut its doors for good on May 8, 2000, when the last woman left.

Kingston's closure was meant to mark a move toward the new values outlined by the "Creating Choices" document. As the title suggests, it said new values would help create choices for women inmates, operating under the premise they would then be better functioning members in the community upon their release. "Creating Choices" identified key problems facing federally-sentenced women: they were among those who had most suffered from sexism, racism, physical and sexual abuse, plus poor education and employment. The report's authors concluded these women didn't need more punitive measures, but empowerment, programs, and work options to take responsibility for their lives inside prison—positive behaviour that would ideally extend beyond prison life. In addition to promoting rehabilitative-focussed programming, the report declared women were housed with little access to fresh air, light, and social interaction, all detrimental factors to healthy rehabilitation.

When Grand Valley first opened, things were optimistic. It embodied the five principles of "Creating Choices" (empowerment, meaningful and responsible choices, respect and dignity, a supportive environment, and shared responsibility), right down to the cottage-style buildings, where a woman's children and family could come and live for extended visits. Back then, it only housed 64 women. For incarcerated women's advocates, it was a much needed change for Canada. "It opened under a whole new vision for how correction for women in Canada was going to operate," says Father Con O'Mahony, a former Grand Valley chaplain. "It was geared towards a much more integrated experience for the woman." One, he adds, that worked well for the first few years.

O'Mahony finally left Grand Valley in 2009, after spending 13 years watching its once great plans disintegrate. He first began to see things change after the federal Conservative government began to implement the first wave of "tough on crime" policies in the mid-2000s. O'Mahony became further disquieted when he noticed inmates' mental health issues had begun to largely be addressed through medication, and nothing else. Then, there was the overcrowding—and worse. Programming was cut. In 2010, the inmates at Grand Valley filed over 120 formal complaints with the Official of the Correctional Investigator, more than any other women's prison in Canada. In 2012, the Conservative government sliced $295 million from CSC's overall budget over a two year period. But, there were little things, too.

Guards who once wore casual clothes came dressed in dark navy uniforms. They began to carry what O'Mahony says looked like tasers. Before things started to change, he was buzzed through only one door before entering a main area where women would approach to talk. "I think it encouraged adults to be adults and it encouraged adult conversation," he says. Now though, there are two levels of security before reaching the entry area. Everybody gets screened. When he went in for mass, often his Bible or his identification were swabbed for drugs. "It was a very different feel," he says. Now, a disoriented Grand Valley has lost its sense of direction and is heading backwards, fast—taking most of its female inmates along with it.

BEFORE SHE WAS an inmate, Ava cross-country skied along Sudbury trails. She studied religious studies at Laurentian University. She made gift baskets to sell in the café she co-owned with her boyfriend. But these are the highlights. When I first met her in October, Ava described her life as "dark and bleak" but left it there. Seven months later, she fills in her story. "I had several experiences of sexual abuse starting from the age of four." She notes that the majority of incarcerated women have been sexually abused—that's a common theme. "To be brutally honest, yes I mean rape."

Her relationship with the boyfriend who she owned the café with started in her mid-20s and lasted roughly five years. It became violent in the early stages. Ava's mother was also abused. So was her grandmother. Still, Ava says she found her place in the café, and loved it. She got along well with the customers and liked making their gift baskets. But slowly, the abuse became too much. She left the relationship and, shortly after, her northern Ontario town, heading to Toronto for a fresh start. But things continued to go in the same direction. "I'd escape from one abusive relationship to another and leave with nothing but the clothes on my back and try to start over," she says. "Eventually I just kind of gave up." In one of our interviews, she tells me it feels like it was inevitable for her life to go in the direction it did, but then adds: "what's different for me is that I was able to move past it."

In Toronto, Ava got a reputation for being impulsive. She moved to the city at age 30. There were times when she abandoned her apartment, not giving her lease a second thought. She got involved in another abusive relationship. She kicked him out; he stole everything from her. He was a con man and had ripped off a lot of people already. "They came looking for him and raped and beat me. I got evicted from my apartment."

From there, Ava turned to crime for the first time. In 2001, she started selling cocaine, then got into sex work, then started using the cocaine to recover from the sex work, then made her way to heroin which she both used and sold. At one point, right before she got arrested, she tried to pull away from her lifestyle and had even started making gift baskets again. But just a few months after she was arrested for selling drugs to an undercover police officer and possessing firearms. Found guilty, she was sentenced to five years in prison. After a year, she was released on early parole. She returned to crime and violated her order within days. "I was like, 'I don't give a shit,'" she says. "Everyone's told me I'm a piece of shit so that's what I am and that's what I'll continue to be." After her parole violation, she was sentenced to an additional three years and four months.

"I work hard to achieve things and then I just fuck them up," Ava says. "While I've been impulsive, I've also been the kind who likes to lay down roots and build things. I'm self-destructive and destroy them, which probably led to the impulsivity...That's why I have this tattoo." She rolls up her sleeve and inscribed in cursive is a message about not tearing down what you've built for yourself. She got it in Grand Valley.

AVA'S FIRST STOP on the way to Grand Valley was the Vanier Centre for Women, a provincial jail in Milton, Ont. If a sentence is less than two years, a person stays in a provincial jail, but many women are also held in custody in a provincial jail as they await their sentence. Ava lived in the high security area of Vanier from March 2009–March 2011 before being transferred.

"It's actually so scary," she says. The first time she entered the doors of Vanier she says, women were in her face: "What have you got? Do you have a package?" They meant drugs. In provincial jail, there's no methadone treatment. You wait until you get out or get to federal prison. On her first stay, Ava walked past plenty of women who were throwing up or had diarrhea. Withdrawal. It's a dirty place. There is no soap for your hands. When someone left the bathroom, someone else would say, "so and so's been smoking crack again." Some women tucked drugs into their bodies; other women knocked them out in the shower to get them. One day, while being escorted out of the high security range to visit a social worker, a guard looked at her and said, "She's a fucking waste of time."

Every day for every meal, she would line up for a spoon. She lined up to give it back. She usually didn't hand it back. Instead, she stuck it through a hatch. Most guards wouldn't touch it, but some would take it from her with a glare. At night, she would go back her cell, back to her mattress on the floor. Clean laundry was still dirty. Sometimes, there would be no socks for a week. The metal door with the slot for meals stayed shut. "It's a relief when you get to Grand Valley," she says. "Believe it or not."

IN GRAND VALLEY, Ava lived in a unit with 10 women. Everyone at the prison receives a food budget of $35.56 per week. While there, Ava would make her list and then another woman picked up the items at the prison's industrial food area. On a typical day, she would wake up at 5:30 or 6 a.m., make breakfast, and go to work. During her time there, she filled a number of positions—librarian, photographer, and member of the inmate committee. She received a release to work at the Humane Society. The highest a woman can earn at Grand Valley is just shy of $7 per day, a wage that has been static since 1981. Pay is situation-dependent and can be as low as $1 per day. Women use the wages to buy basic hygiene needs and pay phone fees to call family. (Just this past fall though, a new rule was established requiring inmates to give 30 percent of their pay back for room and board.) Ava likes buying shoes. She would save her $6 daily wage for months and months, eventually picking the exact right pair from the prison's Nike catalogue.

While many women at Grand Valley worked, others slept away their sentences, she says. At Grand Valley, there is a 90-day evaluation period before an inmate can be entered in core programming. Oftentimes, though, there's a waiting list for programming as well, and there is no guarantee a woman will start programming after the evaluation period. Inmates cannot apply for parole until the programming is complete. Ava has seen women begin their mandatory programming so late, they miss their chance to do so. "The beds are staying full," she says, "and nobody's moving."

The work day for inmates lasts the full morning. After work, Ava would head back to her unit in time for the guards' regular 11:15 a.m. headcount. Ava's clearance came each day at about 12:30 p.m. From there, she went to programs until 4 p.m. Then, another count. It cleared at 5:30 p.m. After that, free time until 9 p.m. Ava would usually head to the gym. "That was my sanity place," she says. "That's what I loved to do." In the beginning they had a weight room, but it was later turned into a guard's office. At one point, there was a step aerobics class. The steps broke, but they used them that way anyway—until they got taken away. Eventually the women received a new shipment of cardio equipment: one elliptical, two treadmills, and two bikes. Ava says the women fought over them constantly. Sometimes Ava would watch TV after. Inmates are allowed 15-inch sets in their cells. They have to pay for cable, whether they have a TV or not.

At Grand Valley, there was one thing that Ava could use to move herself forward. Ava had started a degree in 1992, but says she quit one credit short of graduating. Initially, she just wanted to finish that credit, and decided to take a women's studies course through correspondence. "Then I was like, 'Hey, I would really like to continue studying this.' So I had to do 36 credits in women's studies." While many of Grand Valley's once-big ambitions have shrunk, it still offers post-secondary correspondence courses through Laurentian University, as well as the Inside-Out program. Facilitated by Wilfrid Laurier University in the case of Grand Valley, the program trains professors from across Canada to go into institutions to teach a class that is a mixture of students from the university and students from the prison.

Inside-Out started in the US in 1997 and runs in 25 states. It started in Grand Valley in 2011 with 10 "outside"

students and 7 "inside" students. The program offers courses through the faculty of social work and the faculty of arts
at Wilfrid Laurier and receives funding from the Lyle S.
Hallman Foundation, which gives grants to support education and children's initiatives in the Waterloo region. Wilfrid Laurier University provides texts and bursaries for incarcerated students. For Ava, it was intimidating, especially
her first day of class. "On our end," she says, "we're like 'Oh
my God these are university students, they are going to
think we're dumb.'"

She also worried the students would notice she only had
blue, stained institute T-shirts to wear. What about her
pants? Would these students judge her for wearing the same
ones every week? "Sometimes it sounds really vain, my worries in there," she says. "It makes you feel like you stand out
and all you want to do is just blend in." Her worries didn't
turn into reality. She began to look forward to her Inside-
Out classes every week. Inmate students didn't want class
to end and for the outside students to leave. "It was really
over and above anything we had hoped for," she says. And
between those classes and her correspondence courses, she
managed to finish her degree and graduate on June 8, 2013.
"It felt absolutely amazing," she says. "I am the only woman
in the history of GVI to have completed a degree while being there."

AVA WAS RELEASED from Grand Valley on May 22, 2013.
She went into prison with few chances for a successful future—and doesn't downplay her degree. "Unless you're released from prison and learn something new, you're exactly where you started," she says. "The fact that I was able to
work on my degree, get involved in Inside-Out, I'm now in
college full-time—that's given me all the direction I needed

to try and change. If none of that happened, I don't know what I'd be doing right now. I really don't know." That might make it seem like Creating Choices is still alive. Not quite.

"The GVI that opened in 1997 is not the GVI we have today," says O'Mahony. Ava points to one, big roadblock on the way to education: if women at Grand Valley want to take university correspondence courses, they have to find a way to finance them—something that's incredibly difficult to do on a salary of less than $7 a day. At one point, inmates could get an Ontario Student Assistance Program (OSAP) bursary called Ontario Special Bursaries which awarded a student up to $2,500. Those were last offered for the 2010-2011 year though before they were cut from the Ontario budget. Before the bursaries were cancelled, says Ava, 30 women were studying post-secondary inside Grand Valley via correspondence. The next year, that number dropped to two. Ava paid for school through scholarships, a $500 grant from the Elizabeth Fry Association (a group that helps incarcerated women) and a different grant from OSAP.

Outside of Grand Valley, Ava says she's lonely, that she has no friends, and has only been to the movies once. She's not allowed to talk to anyone from prison because she's on parole. She feels displaced. Prices have changed. Muffins used to be $1, now they are $2. She took a trip to Shoppers Drug Mart recently, but left. The tattoo underneath her sleeve is a reminder to stay on course. She talks about these things and about her life of abuse and drugs and her women's studies degree that she had to fight so hard for inside a penitentiary that has become hardened and strict. Somewhere on a bridge above the Don Valley River on our way to her boxing class, she stops and says "I like walking across bridges."

Before we walk through the gym's doors, she stops again and tells me she's wearing two pairs of pants. She says quickly, her tone hushed: "It's a habit from prison," where the cells were cold and an extra pair of pants meant an extra layer of protection between her skin and filth. Months later, she tells me she's always worried that something will send her back to Grand Valley—that everything she's worked for is all hanging together by a string and that it could snap so easily. Sometimes in the city, she comes face-to-face with women from her prison days, still stuck in the cycle.

The other boxers don't know about Grand Valley yet (although, tired of living a double life, she will later tell them). During the workout she's smiling, making wisecracks. "It looks easier than it is," she says, even though she jumps at the chance to use the weighted ball. With every exercise she adds a twist making it more challenging. The gym blasts OutKast's "Hey Ya!" and has a brown-haired, freckle-faced coach who says that every woman needs a heavy bag to punch. "Better out than in," she says. Throughout the gym the sound of gloves hitting and bouncing off punching bags echo. Here, at least, Ava moves with ease.

The Jihadists of Suburbia

Naheed Mustafa

RAED JASER WAS 15 years old when he and his family arrived in Toronto in 1993. During the Gulf War, his Palestinian parents, Mohammed and Sabah, had been forced to leave the United Arab Emirates. Mohammed worked as an ad sales rep at a newspaper and had refused to give in to Emirati government agents' demands that he spy on other Palestinians. To avoid persecution, the Jasers headed to Czechoslovakia, then to Germany and finally to Canada. With them were Raed's younger brothers, 11-year-old Nabil and 10-year-old Shadi. And Sabah Jaser was some five months' pregnant with another boy. The immigration officer who interviewed the family noted in their file that their refugee case should be sorted out as soon as possible, before the baby was born.

The Immigration and Refugee Board didn't believe the family's story and rejected their claim, but four years later they were accepted under a now-defunct program that allowed refugee claimants to stay if they were stateless and therefore had no country to be deported to. Raed, however, didn't qualify: while his parents were navigating the refugee system, he'd earned a criminal record. In 1997, he was convicted of fraud offences totalling more than $15,000, for various big-ticket items, including a gas oven and sound equipment. He ignored the order to leave the country. Two years later, still living in the GTA, he was arrested again, this time for uttering a death threat to a manager of a Richmond Hill pub. He was sentenced to two years' probation and fined $1,000.

His continued run-ins with the law eventually caught the attention of immigration authorities, and in 2004 a warrant was issued for his arrest. He was detained at the Toronto West Detention Centre, but, again, there was no obvious place to deport him to. A court official decided he should be released until immigration authorities could figure out where to send him. His uncle, Mahmoud Jaser, paid a $3,000 cash bond.

Jaser straightened out his life and, five years later, was issued a pardon from the Parole Board of Canada, which allowed him to pursue permanent resident status. He received that in 2012. He was 32 years old.

Jaser founded a limousine company and got married. His wife is a practising Muslim, like him. She is strict about covering and wears a niqab. They lived in an apartment in a house on Cherokee Boulevard in North York and kept to themselves. She would accompany Jaser to pray at mosques but rarely interacted with anyone.

In 2011, the limo business failed, and Jaser got a job driving a minivan part-time for a private transportation company in Markham, ferrying special-ed students to and from Unionville High School. He also worked as a customer service rep for a North York moving company.

He spent most of his spare time at suburban mosques, including the Jam'e Masjid in Markham, which is colloquially known as Middlefield for the road it sits on. The mosque is large and white, with arched windows and traditional domes and minarets. The people who attend it are mostly middle-class South Asian-Canadians who live nearby.

At Middlefield, Jaser would often spend his free time proselytizing to other Muslims. It seems an odd thing—preaching to those already praying—but it's not uncommon among devout Muslims. You may already be an observant Muslim, but you can always use a boost to stay on the right track. When he wasn't proselytizing, he'd watch YouTube lectures given by celebrity scholars and preachers like Abdur Raheem Green, Bilal Philips and Farhat Hashmi. Their lectures are not unlike the kinds of sermons a conservative Christian might hear at a megachurch—a mix of scripture and motivational talk about how to live a moral life by applying religious principles to everyday problems. Part history lesson, part advice, part fear of God's wrath, all wrapped up in a slick production.

In 2010, Jaser met a man at Middlefield who shared his obsessions. Chiheb Esseghaier, then a 28-year-old Tunisian doctoral student at the Université du Québec, specialized in nanotechnology and biosensors. He had a full beard, an intense gaze behind metal-rimmed glasses and the withdrawn personality of a bookworm. Even though they came from very different backgrounds, they fell into long conversations about religion, politics and Esseghaier's studies.

Esseghaier began visiting Jaser in Toronto, often crashing at his home. He never spoke to Jaser's wife even though she was in the apartment. (Which isn't that unusual: in Jaser and Esseghaier's strict interpretation of the Muslim faith, men and women who are unrelated simply do not interact.) The men talked about how they believed Muslims were oppressed by the West. They talked about how wrong it was that Canada had troops in Afghanistan with the NATO mission. NATO, in Esseghaier's view, was intent on colonizing the country and forcing secularism upon Muslims.

He wanted to send Canadians a message.

IF YOU LIKE to debate the ethics of Canada fighting a war in Afghanistan or bombing Libya or, most recently, participating in the fight in Iraq, you'd better not do it at a mosque. Since the attacks of 9/11, mosques in the GTA have been routinely monitored by the RCMP and CSIS. Imams and mosque managers are expected and encouraged to monitor for extremist behaviour, and it's no secret that informants regularly attend mosques. Some mosque boards are so concerned about even a whiff of extremism that they are quick to cut off any and all political discussion on the premises.

The management in at least two mosques, including Jam'e Masjid, asked Jaser to stop proselytizing and suggested that he should find somewhere else to worship. His zealousness made people uncomfortable.

Several sources told me that Said Rageah, then the imam at the Abu Huraira mosque in North York, tipped off the RCMP about Jaser. Abu Huraira is the same mosque that was in the news in 2009, cited as the place where five young Somali-Canadian men prayed before disappearing and allegedly joining al Shabab, the al Qaeda affiliate in Somalia.

When I called Rageah, who now runs the Sakinah Center (which provides social services and helps at-risk youth), I asked if he tipped off the RCMP, but he refused to comment. When I pressed him, he lost his cool and hung up.

Mohammed Jaser asked Muhammad Robert Heft, another prominent community leader, to provide counsel to Raed, who had become morally rigid. Heft is tall and solidly built, with a full red beard. He was born into a Lutheran family and raised in Milton, and converted to Islam in

1998. He collaborates with the RCMP and CSIS to deradicalize Muslim youth. He also runs an organization called P4E—Paradise Forever—which provides social services in Scarborough to new Muslims. He's known for having served as a court-appointed counsellor to Steven Chand, a member of the Toronto 18 who was convicted in 2010 of trying to raise funds for the group. In 2010, Mohammed Jaser happened to be renting an apartment in Heft's house in Markham. He knew Heft was the go-to guy on extremism and asked him to speak to Raed, who had grown intolerant and self-righteous, even criticizing the length of Mohammed's beard. But Mohammed Jaser never followed through, and Heft soon forgot about the request.

In early 2012, Chiheb Esseghaier applied for a US visa at the embassy in Ottawa. He was to speak on the use of biosensors in HIV diagnosis at a conference in Santa Clara, California, in June of that year. During his visa interview, he mentioned having travelled twice to Zahedan, a city in Iran close to both the Pakistani and Afghan borders. The Iran trip raised a red flag for the RCMP and the FBI.

He was granted a visa nevertheless, and on the flight to Santa Clara sat next to a man named Tamer El Noury, who introduced himself as an Egyptian-American businessman based in Manhattan and specializing in real estate. El Noury asked about Esseghaier's studies, and they talked about religion and politics. Before the end of the flight they traded phone numbers, promising to stay in touch. Once Esseghaier was back in Canada, El Noury arranged to visit him in Montreal, where they went for dinner and Esseghaier introduced his new friend to Ahmed Abassi, a 25-year-old fellow PhD student from Tunisia with a short, neatly trimmed beard. In Toronto, Esseghaier later introduced El Noury to Raed Jaser.

Right away, Jaser liked El Noury, who was charming and confident and spoke of his commitment to fighting for God's cause. He and Esseghaier felt like they could trust him. They told their wealthy new friend that they were sickened by the war in Afghanistan—that they wanted NATO out of all Muslim countries. According to the RCMP, they'd decided to derail a passenger train. Trains are an easy target—there is little if any security along train tracks, and they're often surrounded by open fields. The way to cause the most damage and draw the most attention to their cause, they figured, was to sabotage the track on a railway bridge. They'd identified one near Jordan Station, just west of St. Catharines. The Maple Leaf, which is run by Via and Amtrak, travels over it en route to Penn Station in New York. After hearing about their plan, El Noury gave Jaser $1,000 to purchase video equipment.

In September 2012, someone spotted Jaser and Esseghaier checking out the tracks, and called the police. After that trip, Jaser decided to return the $1,000 to El Noury. He told Esseghaier he was done—he didn't want any part of the plan. He wanted to start a business, maybe a restaurant, and have a normal life. Esseghaier was furious. He never spoke to Jaser again.

ESSEGHAIER AND JASER didn't know that Tamer El Noury was an FBI agent. He was taping his conversations with the men, and the FBI was in contact with the RCMP and CSIS. His assignment was to gather evidence that the men were plotting a terror attack.

The FBI frequently plants informants in mosques, and has been criticized by defence lawyers and legal experts for entrapping Muslim men by encouraging them to plot terror acts. Since 9/11, dozens of US terrorism investigations have involved informants, including the arrest of four men in Newburgh, New York, who were convicted of plotting to bomb a synagogue and shoot down military planes. According to their defence lawyer, the informant "proposed, directed, supplied, funded and facilitated every aspect of the 'terrorist' plot," even promising payments of $250,000 and luxury cars, and providing them with the fake bombs that got them arrested.

Similar methods appear to have been used by the FBI in their interactions with Esseghaier and his associates. El Noury was convinced Esseghaier's Tunisian friend Ahmed Abassi was a partner in the same terror plot, but he needed proof. El Noury decided to lure Abassi and Esseghaier to New York, where he'd talk to them about their plans and record their conversations. Abassi had left Canada for Tunisia in December 2012 to visit family. There, the Canadian government revoked his visa. From the US, El Noury kept up a steady stream of phone calls and emails to Abassi, trying to convince him that he should just come to New York. El Noury would take care of a US visa and a place to stay, and help him sort out his Canadian visa problems. Abassi agreed and flew to New York in March 2013 on a visa arranged, unbeknownst to him, by the FBI. Over the next few weeks, Esseghaier visited the two men at a luxurious Manhattan apartment near Wall Street, ostensibly owned by El Noury.

El Noury, Abassi and Esseghaier, talking in Arabic, debated the pros and cons of a variety of terror schemes. They squabbled over the best approach. Abassi had many ideas to share, including contaminating the air or water with bacteria to potentially kill 100,000 people. They talked about Esseghaier's visits to Iran, where he claimed to have met al Qaeda point men who advised him to recruit people but lie low until he was needed.

At one point, alone with El Noury, Esseghaier complained that Abassi wasn't fully committed to their cause and argued that they needed to cut him out of their plans. Esseghaier compared him to Jaser, who wasn't initially afraid but "got afraid later." He claimed that Jaser only participated so he could get some money from El Noury to start a restaurant.

THE US AND Canadian investigators had the evidence they needed to bring charges. On April 22, Ahmed Abassi was arrested in New York and charged with fraudulently applying for a US visa to facilitate an act of international terrorism. That same day, the RCMP held a press conference at its facility near Pearson airport. To a room of TV cameras, James Malizia, an RCMP assistant commissioner, announced that Raed Jaser and Chiheb Esseghaier had been arrested and charged with conspiring to carry out a terrorist act against a Via passenger train. Jaser had been apprehended by 15 officers while at work at a North York moving company, and Esseghaier was picked up while working on a laptop at a McDonald's in Montreal's central train station. Malizia said the two had received direction from al Qaeda operatives in Iran. The charges were sensational, especially coming only a week after the bombing of the Boston Marathon.

The RCMP invited 23 leaders and imams from the GTA's Muslim community to the facility, and asked them to be available to the media after the press conference. Muhammad Robert Heft was one of those in attendance. He told me he was not at all surprised by the charges against Jaser and Esseghaier. "With the right propaganda, the right kind of circumstances, loose cannons are easily radicalized," he said.

This past March, Heft went to see Jaser in jail. During his visit, Jaser said he was only going along with Esseghaier's plans in hopes of convincing him not to do it. Jaser claimed he was trying to wean him away from the plan. Heft told Jaser he didn't buy that excuse. "He shot back and said 'Well, I don't have to convince you,' and I said, 'If you can't convince me, you won't be able to convince a judge.'"

"My hope would be Raed owns up to what he says in the taped evidence and pleads guilty," Heft told me. "Instead of going after him for life in prison, maybe the court will give him a few years in jail, and then he can come out and speak to people and say, look, this is wrong, nobody should think like this."

Heft told me how someone tried to recruit him just a few years after he converted to Islam. He says he was a good target because even though he'd been Muslim for a handful of years, he was made to feel like an outsider by the community. His newfound mentor, someone he would only describe as an older Egyptian man, convinced him that everyone in the Muslim community was wrong, and that he, Heft, was among the chosen few who really understood what Islam was. Young men are easily radicalized, he says, if you convince them they're destined for extraordinary things.

I HAVE MY own indirect connection to Raed Jaser. My husband's friend Umar, whom he's known since their elementary school days in Karachi, had met Jaser in 2007 at Middlefield. He was surprised by Jaser's arrest.

When Umar, who doesn't want his last name used, first came to Canada, he wasn't particularly religious. As the years went by, he became more observant; he grew his beard long, and, like Jaser, the only thing he liked to talk about was Islam. Umar initially approached Jaser asking if he'd help him improve his Arabic, and the two would often travel together to mosques, to pray and proselytize. Umar says Jaser would get angry and frustrated when people didn't pay attention to his impromptu lectures, but Umar would tell him that spreading the message of Islam required patience.

One day, Jaser introduced Umar to Chiheb Esseghaier and asked if he could put Chiheb up in his apartment in the Thorncliffe Park neighbourhood. Esseghaier stayed overnight but mostly kept to himself.

The day after the arrests of Esseghaier and Jaser, Umar was stopped at a takeout restaurant by two men who identified themselves as CSIS agents. They took him back to the RCMP's facility near the airport for an interview. The agents told him they had recordings of his conversations with Jaser. "They asked me about my views on jihad and what Raed's view was," he said. "I explained that I didn't know what Raed thought, but in my view jihad is something everyone should be doing: jihad is about helping and struggling. If someone falls, you assist them."

Umar told me Jaser never spoke to him about terrorism or violent plans. He says the man he knew was very helpful. If someone was unemployed or needed money or advice about paperwork, Jaser would offer his time in any way he could. "The CSIS agents asked me if he ever talked about trains or anything, and I said no.

"We used to talk about our future, and he used to say we'd open a restaurant," Umar said. "I told him I would be an employee, not a partner, because I don't know about these things. He said we could use our business as a way to help needy people by making money from it and spending it on others." Jaser had even scouted a location for the business.

In December of last year, Umar asked my husband for a ride to the airport to catch a flight to Pakistan to see his sick mother. When they got there, Umar was taken aside by security: he was on a US watch list. He could fly, but not through American airspace. They wouldn't tell him anything more. He later found out it was because of his friendship with Jaser.

THE AMERICAN LEGAL proceedings against Ahmed Abassi moved more swiftly than the Canadian case against Jaser and Esseghaier. As part of a plea deal, the federal prosecutors withdrew the terrorism charges, and Abassi, who admitted to a role in radicalizing Esseghaier, pleaded guilty to immigration fraud. Abassi's lawyer argued that he had been entrapped by El Noury, who drew him to the US under false pretenses. Abassi was ultimately sentenced to time served—15 months—and deported to Tunisia.

In Toronto, Chiheb Esseghaier has been steadfast in his refusal to participate in his own case. He told the court over and over that he would only accept a lawyer who could defend him using sharia law. He appeared at his hearings in an orange jumpsuit, his long beard and curly hair dishevelled. He explained to the judge that he refused to be tried under Canada's Criminal Code because man-made laws were inferior to God's laws as embodied in the Quran. He complained that the Criminal Code protected gay marriage and was therefore an abomination, and he protested when a female court officer moved to handcuff him. "You are not my wife," he said.

Raed Jaser did his best to distance himself from Esseghaier. He secured a civil liberties criminal lawyer named John Norris, who had represented Omar Khadr and a member of the Toronto 18. Jaser's family attended his first court appearances and refused to speak to journalists.

The post-9/11 conviction rate for terrorism cases that go

to trial is close to 100 per cent. Defence lawyers say that in these types of cases they must overcome the impression that the accused is guilty until proven innocent. Norris declined my requests for an interview, though he stated that his client denies the allegations categorically. I approached Rocco Galati, a Toronto lawyer who represented Abdurahman Khadr, Omar's older brother, as well as another suspect in the Toronto 18 plot, to ask what it's like to represent someone facing charges like Jaser's. He told me such cases are always "loaded against the accused" and that in few other cases would the kind of evidence submitted in these trials pass muster. Galati says the wiretap evidence often consists of sections of audio, and the undercover agent or informant is the one who provides context and explains what came before and after the section in question. In that sense, he says, the evidence is "manufactured."

John Norris also refused my request for a meeting with Raed Jaser, saying he wasn't giving interviews. Chiheb Esseghaier, however, agreed to see me. We met at the Toronto West Detention Centre in Etobicoke, in a large room with dozens of booths where inmates and visitors sat across from each other separated by Plexiglas dividers. He had the same dishevelled look I saw in court.

I asked Esseghaier about his split from Jaser. He started lecturing me about colonization and media conspiracies. I stopped taking notes. "Why aren't you writing this down?" he demanded. I told him I would write only if he answered my question. He tried to pick up where he left off, and I let my pen lie on my notebook. "Okay, okay," he said. "Raed Jaser turned his back on the Holy Quran. He ran to the Criminal Code to accept the human law. Why did he do that? Before, we were friends, but now I am criticizing that behaviour." He carried on: "When Muslims see the wrong thing they need to advise Muslims to do the right thing. Raed Jaser did something wrong when he accepted the human law."

Esseghaier's core goal—he insisted I write it down—is that "the whole world is united in a single state and ruled under the rules in the Quran." That's what he sees as his life's work. Everything he says and does is in the service of that end. When I pressed him to clarify details of his "plots" and "schemes," he became agitated. He said *he* is not the story, and what *he* did or didn't do is not the point. "I am just a detail of a detail," he said. "The fact that I was going to the bridge or going to the railway track by St. Catharines isn't relevant. And these small plans that I was making are the striving and the struggling to realize the bigger plan."

The trial is set to begin sometime in early 2015, and the two men face life sentences. The case relies heavily on wire-taps and surveillance spanning nearly a year. The timelines of alleged offences are short—in the case of Raed Jaser, just a few months. Esseghaier still does not have a lawyer and refuses to even recognize the criminal justice system. But he seems undisturbed by his situation. His goal, he says, is a higher one. "Everything I did in Canada, I hope God will see that as a sincere effort to help His cause," he told me. In my last interview with Esseghaier, I asked him if he is concerned about his future. He wonders about what will happen to him and his case, but he believes the outcome is out of his hands. "God plans everything and then makes it all possible," he said. "No one will escape his destiny."

Brazil Diary:
Drones, Favelas, Docs and Football

JASON O'HARA

JULY 13, 2014, Rio de Janeiro. The Argentine and German football squads are preparing to face off in the FIFA World Cup finals. Mostly international tourists will be attending today's match while the majority of Brazilians will watch from television screens outside. But some Brazilians won't be watching the game at all; instead they're taking to the streets to exercise their constitutionally guaranteed right to protest. It is not mere opportunism that brings them to the streets, seeking to capitalize on all the attention garnered by the Cup. Their grievances are very much tied to the international spectacle and the social legacy it will leave in this country. When the circus leaves town, it is Brazilians who will bear the brunt of the hangover, sifting through the trash to recover all the discarded beer cans after the party.

Donning a Canadian military gas mask and bright yellow Activist helmet from Mountain Equipment Co-op, I am in the eye of the storm, the Saens Peña square, one mile from the iconic Maracanã Stadium and ground zero for today's protest. I am in Rio continuing production on my first feature-length documentary about forced evictions in advance of the 2014 World Cup and 2016 Olympics.

Police have quarantined activists and media alike, using the same kettling tactic we saw police using in Toronto during the G20, when I was in the streets shooting my first short documentary, *Demur*. No one is permitted to enter the square and no one may leave. The memory card in my camera fills up and I press myself against a wall to change it. A line of military police are running by and one swings his baton my way, an indication to all successive police in line that I must be one of the terrorists they have been looking for and I am soon taking blows from all sides. I drop to the floor, batons continuing to crash down on me. One of the officers rips off the GoPro camera affixed to my helmet, and another swoops in for the final blow, a swift boot to the chops. As I am whisked away to the hospital in an ambulance, I cannot help but ask myself: How on earth did I end up here?

The answer to that is a long story.

IT IS 2010, and I'm returning to Brazil, a country I fell in love with after living in the cities of Recife and Belo Horizonte between 2006 and 2008. I am in Rio to co-present a film I co-directed with Canadian documentary filmmaker Tom Radford, *Cities Crossing Borders*. Rio is hosting the 5th UN Habitat World Urban Forum. We have been invited to present our feature-length film, and show a 20-minute version at the opening ceremonies on nine large screens before 8,000 guests gathered from around the globe, including Brazil's President Lula and several other heads of state. We have a captive audience and are pleased for the opportunity to set the tone for the week's prestigious event with our hard-hitting film about the crises facing megacities, the supposed focus of the event.

As the room fills up and the film's opening sequence

rolls, the cheery samba music that has been serenading the arrival of delegates all morning never fades, and our film plays start-to-finish as a silent slideshow. This was no technical glitch: it is evident that the "tone" of our piece was not in keeping with the festive atmosphere event organizers were trying to construct in a bombastic fashion. Our silenced film was a mere prelude to the extensive song-and-dance that would follow, a full-on "Carnaval" procession mounted to welcome all the international delegates to the so-called "marvellous city" of Rio. This was my first experience with censorship in Brazil but it would not be my last.

Angry and disappointed, we exited the Lula event and walked across the street to the parallel gathering being organized by Brazilian civil society, the World Social Forum. It was a revelation to be there. While not much of a sports fan, I must admit my affinity for the World Cup and Olympics, perhaps duped by all the rhetoric of FIFA's (Fédération Internationale de Football Association) "beautiful game" and the values of the Olympic charter. My naïve appreciation for these events was quickly undermined by everything I heard at the forum. Despite the stereotype that all Brazilians are crazy about football, the ones I met were deeply concerned about the potential social impacts of these events, particularly in Rio, where the two mega-spectacles would be hosted back to back in 2014 and 2016.

The Brazilians told me that when FIFA and the IOC (International Olympic Committee) come to town, a "state of exception" is imposed: a legal framework that temporarily suspends the rule of law and strangles civil liberties such as the right to free movement and protest. Since 2010, thousands of families have been forcefully displaced, despite unambiguous international laws prohibiting such displacement. The "state of exception" is justified by the expediency needed to prepare for the World Cup and the Olympics, time-sensitive events that cannot be jeopardized by the potential delays of due legal process.

I returned to Canada tremendously concerned for the fate of Brazil. I started researching past Olympics and World Cups and what I discovered was appalling. I learned about the role hosting the 2004 Olympics played in precipitating Greece's successive debt crises, the thousands of poor displaced and relocated to unliveable tin shacks in South Africa for the 2010 World Cup, and here in Canada, where the epic 1976 games, bid at a total price of $120 million, ended up costing $1.5 billion, leaving Montreal indebted for 30 years. (All this after the Montreal mayor Jean Drapeau famously declared, "The Olympics can no more have a deficit than a man can have a baby.")

Wide-eyed idealism is not uncommon in the mega-events' bid processes. Since 1976, the average cost overrun for the Olympics has exceeded 200 per cent. As event critic Helen Lenskyj so aptly summarizes: "These projects, massive in their scope and scale, cost many billions of public dollars and leave behind ambiguous legacies. Nearly every global mega-event has resulted in financial losses for the host, temporary cessation of democratic process, the production of militarized and exclusionary spaces, residential displacement and environmental degradation."

Having lived in Brazil twice before and knowing what I did of the socio-political context in that country—a new democracy emerging from a totalitarian dictatorship with high levels of corruption in both the private and public sphere—I realized that the country was heading into a crisis. But I also knew that the pending social catastrophe was hardly a *fait accompli*; on the contrary, Brazilian civil society boasted some of the world's most effective political organizers.

It is no coincidence the World Social Forum was born in Brazil, in Porto Alegre in 2001 under the guiding principle that "another world is possible." Social movements from all corners of the globe gathered for the first time at what would become an annual international gathering. There were no leaders nor unifying ideology; in their place was vehement disagreement as to what that "possible other world" might look like. It was pure democracy in all of its messiness. Brazil is also home to the Landless Workers' Movement (MST), one of the world's most successful and widely studied social movements, and to Paulo Freire, whose *Pedagogy of the Oppressed* asserted the democratic power of the world's marginalized classes.

In Rio, many of Brazil's marginalized people live in the favelas. Historically, the favelas emerged in marginal unliveable hillsides, public lands that were settled by rural migrants flooding to the city to provide the labour for Brazil's industrial boom throughout the 20th century. Brazilian *usucapio* laws formalized squatters' rights and allowed acquisition of land through unchallenged possession for a specified number of years (usually ten). After the decline of the dictatorship, which had lasted from the 1960s to the mid '80s, in acknowledgement of the tremendous sacrifice made by the labouring class, favela residents' right to housing was strengthened even further. A constitutional clause was passed that guaranteed land ownership as a fundamental right, and required that all land serve a social function. It's this very same clause utilized by the MST that has been used to successfully reclaim lands from Brazil's plutocracy. The clause is perhaps the world's most progressive example of formal squatters' rights guaranteed by a nation's constitution.

Since the dictatorship lost power in the mid '80s, populist

elements in Brazilian civil society had been readying themselves for a showdown with the neo-liberals and oligarchies that ruled the nation. Under Lula, who started his political career with radical rhetoric but quickly became "establishment," Brazil's economy was booming with global capital flooding into the country. The push to cleanse Rio predated the World Cup, with the growing bourgeoisie desiring to take over the favelas, places for the poor, which were suddenly fancied by the wealthy as real estate speculation in surrounding neighbourhoods boomed.

With the mega-spectacles of the World Cup and the Olympics providing the opportunity that the opportunists had been waiting for, land was being seized and civil rights oppressed. The battleground was set for a series of confrontations. I knew that I needed to tell this story.

In 2010, I was an aspiring filmmaker with little experience and no contacts in Rio, but I spoke Portuguese. I packed my camera, jumped on a flight and started talking to people. It did not take me long to make connections with Rio's social movements. I was an outsider but was warmly received. While I'm no fan of reductionist stereotypes, it is true that Brazil is a very receptive culture, a fact exploited by both FIFA and the IOC.

On this first trip, I awoke one morning to a message that a forced eviction was under way in the west part of Rio in the community of Vila Taboinha. I hightailed it to the location where the community entrance was barricaded: men, women and children were refusing to allow the passage of the bulldozers. It was not long before the state riot police were called in. What happened next has become a tired story: tear gas, rubber bullets, the whole force of the Brazilian state unfurled upon the men, women and children who courageously stood in defence of their community. Despite the brute force, the police were outnumbered and the community defiant, and as the sun set, the police were forced to retreat. It was a small victory, an early coup for the "Davids" of the favelas against the Goliath that is the Brazilian state, with global capital in tow.

Three days later, with most of the community away at work, the police returned, this time with neither the same fierce community resistance nor the media presence of days before. The bulldozers started toppling homes. Working with an activist friend, I started shooting the bulldozer emerging from the rubble where buildings had stood a half-hour earlier.

We were accosted immediately by the police chief, who screamed in my face: "This is not for the world to see!" I begged to differ. The police started antagonizing us and we were quickly surrounded by the community, who rose to our defence, several of them filming the altercation with their cell phones, the new instrument of accountability. The chief was bluffing and we knew it. The intimidation was quickly reversed and the police forced to withdraw. We were quickly ushered away by members of the community who accompanied us from one safe hiding place to another, awaiting the departure of the police.

It was on that day in Vila Taboinha that the documentary project, which is still occupying my life, was born. The community was confronting what seemed like a helpless situation and clearly saw my camera as a glimmer of hope amidst an utterly desperate situation. And I was completely out of my comfort zone, confronting aggressive police threats, totally reliant on the community for my own safety. The incident clearly demonstrated the emerging power of citizen journalism, the new accountability being created by the infallible witnesses that are video and cell-phone cameras.

It also made me realize the necessity of embracing a participatory framework to produce the kind of film I want to make, because the State was clearly going to try and carry out its dirty work away from the peering lens of the media. They never considered that the communities they are seeking to evict may well become media-makers themselves, and I had a feeling this could well be the communities' best defence.

Years earlier, I had organized a series of participatory photography workshops in a number of Brazilian favelas, utilizing a methodology that would later be made famous by the Academy Award-winning documentary *Born into Brothels*, putting creative tools in the hands of the socially marginalized to tell their own stories. Combining Paulo Freire's ideas as they apply to media-making with lessons from the NFB's Challenge for Change programme, our project ethos was born. I began bringing equipment down to a growing network of activists and community residents, most of whom had no experience with video but were keen, and quickly started filming.

The discourse around community video has been constructed around the high ideals of empowerment, participation and democratic control. It has attracted criticism as hyperbole since such ideals are incredibly difficult to achieve in practice. There is a risk that, under the guise of empowerment, the methodology is in fact imperialistic, indenturing participants to a project in which they have no power over the final films.

Such a state of indenture would be antithetical to the very ethos of participatory media. I work with Brazilians and there are no strings attached. Their own media activism shall always come first, the documentary second, if they so choose to participate. I don't own any of their footage—they do. Of course, such an open arrangement cultivates a mutual sense of loyalty. Most participants are very eager to contribute to the documentary, so it is not just a matter of ethics, but also the most strategic approach in terms of securing participation. It's a win-win situation.

One of my earliest collaborators, Patrick Granja, is a journalist writing for the bi-weekly Marxist newspaper based out of Rio: *A Nova Democracia* (*The New Democracy*). Since equipping him with his first camera, he has published 300-plus videos on YouTube, garnering over 24,000 subscribers and 7.2 million channel views. In Patrick's case, our ethos of participant agency has meant building a career as an independent media activist, making a living selling the exclusive footage to international media. And so a lot of our footage is already in the public domain, on YouTube and appearing in news reports and documentaries all over the world on the BBC, VICE News, Al-Jazeera, and many other major media outlets. There have been many horror stories in Rio that would have never seen the light of the media's glare if Patrick hadn't started showing up every time a poor favela dweller was murdered by the police or a community was being evicted from their homes. He publishes all of his stories on YouTube, sometimes journalistic in presentation and other times accompanied by Pat's voice-of-God narration. It has been very interesting to watch Pat's developing aesthetic as he has evolved from simple montages combining witness testimonies and narration, to more sophisticated evidentiary methods i.e., long takes, combining synced split-screen images from our multiple cameras.

When Pat's cell phone rings, my heart always skips a beat. I remember one afternoon in 2012, Pat had a hunch that something serious was going to go down that evening in Complexo de Alemão, an area of 11 favelas in Rio's North Zone, and he asked me to join him on his mission. Visitors to Rio can visit Complexo de Alemão, riding a quarter-billion-dollar gondola (identical to those used at ski resorts) to the heart of the community and back without ever having to disembark. It would not be out of place for there to be a sign posted "Visitors should remember to please keep their hands inside at all times and not feed any of the poor favelados below."

The community was already under military rule in 2012, in a state of transition to the installation of permanent "pacification" police (UPP). On recent nights, some of the military men had been throwing their weight around and antagonizing residents, arbitrarily shutting parties down and even entering homes and helping themselves to residents' food. Hostilities were growing between residents and the military occupiers. We headed up the hill before sunset and sure enough, as night fell, the commotion began immediately and the community descended into riots. Young kids scurried through the alleys with shirts over their faces and rocks in their hands; the fluorescent pink lights of tracer bullets filled the night sky as the military forces were firing live rounds. We were right in the middle of it all for hours and I was terrified but kept on shooting footage. Two residents were killed that night. When we left in the early hours of the morning, we passed through several military blockades. The community was in lockdown. We passed the media scrum at the base of the community, several kilometres from the eye of the storm with all the journalists wearing helmets and bullet-proof vests.

THE NEXT TIME I would return to Alemão was in late 2012, this time to investigate a triple homicide by the newly minted "pacification" police (UPP). "Pacification" is one of those fabulous examples of overt doublespeak not dissimilar from the "freedom" the US military have been bestowing the world over. Initially, "pacification" brought much hope to communities that had long been suffering from the violence associated with criminal gangs and militias. Those hopes were quickly dashed by the egregious abuses of a new gun-toting gang perpetrating summary executions and disappearances, this time with official state sanction.

We were called to Alemão by human rights investigator Márcia Honorato, who was investigating the case of two young boys that had been shot down by a member of the UPP, one of the youth killed point blank, the second wounded but initially still alive. Residents reported that a second UPP officer pleaded with the shooter that they should bring the wounded youth to the police station. The aggressive officer retorted to the other that he better shut his mouth or he was going to end up like these kids, with a bullet in his head. Hours later, both the protesting officer and the surviving boy were found murdered. After her investigation, Honorato concluded that this was a triple homicide. The sequence of events comprises the most horrific scene from my Ryerson's master's thesis film, *Rhythms of Resisitance*, a story about artists in Rio who are protesting against such cases of egregious violence by the UPP in the so-called pacified favelas.

I travelled back and forth from Canada to Rio eight times over the course of four years (from 2010 to 2014), for a total of 32 weeks of production, bringing more and more video gear and growing our collaborative network of video activists on the ground. In June of 2013, on the eve of the FIFA Confederations Cup (the rehearsal for the following summer's spectacle World Cup event), Brazilians took to the streets en masse in what became known as the Brazilian Spring. The initial impetus was a 20 *centavo* (10 cents) hike in transit fares in São Paulo, which might seem inconsequential to most, but to the working poor whose commute often consists of many such buses in a non-integrated transit system, the fare increase was a tipping point that threatened their already precarious economic survival.

It was not the fare hikes but the heavy-handed response by the state that sent Brazilians to the streets en masse, and within days the whole country had erupted in the largest civil uprising in Brazilian history since the 1992 protests calling for the impeachment of President Fernando Collor de Mello. The government quickly reneged on the transit fare increase but it was too late. Brazilians had had a taste of their collective power and their rallying cry quickly became "It's about a lot more than 20 centavos," and much of the discontent was projected on the spectacle events. The grievances being expressed in the streets were multi-fold: thousands of families forcefully evicted from their homes (often brutally, by riot police firing tear gas and rubber bullets); overspending on the football stadiums and other event-related infrastructure, while basic public services such as health care, education and basic sanitation were pitifully underfunded; and the militarization of the favelas in Rio, through the "pacification" program.

One of the largest mobilizations took place for the Confederations Cup finals in Rio at the iconic Maracanã stadium. As the Brazilian squad vanquished Spain 3-0 inside, we were confronted by a scale of repression we had never before seen in the streets outside, dodging rubber bullets and choking on military-grade tear gas. The fact that Brazil's elite football squad was kicking a ball around for the entertainment of the economic elite inside the Maracanã while the military surrounded the stadium to keep the Brazilian populace at bay was the ultimate metaphor for the increasing social exclusion spawned by these mega-events. Since its inauguration for the World Cup in 1950, Maracanã has been a landmark in Brazil, a temple of not just sport and home to much of Pele's illustrious career, but also the location of some of Brazil's most important political rallies. Hosting as many as 200,000 revellers in its heyday, it was the largest stadium on the planet.

Most importantly, Maracanã was thoroughly Brazilian, its very architecture reflecting its accessibility as a popular space. The "best seats in the house" were not seats at all; they were the *geral* section at ground level circumnavigating the field, where the energy was raucous and the chanting deafening. The geral was where the culture of *futebol* thrived. The geral was not just closest to the action, but the tickets were just one Brazilian *real* (50 cents), so accessible even to the poorest citizens, who would often panhandle outside the gates to gain access to the cultural experience inside the most iconic temple of football—Maracanã.

The pressure to reform Maracanã began in the lead-up to the 2007 Pan Am Games, Rio's first big mega-sporting event, a precursor to the city's ambitious event bids to FIFA and the IOC. The stadium was closed for renovations in the lead-up to Pan Am, the geral section eliminated entirely and the first luxury boxes installed. The stadium would close again prior to the World Cup—the capacity was reduced to a mere 78,000 and even more luxury boxes were installed, as per FIFA's stringent stipulations. The Maracanã had been turned into a world-class stadium to host a world-class event, Brazilians be damned. The transformation of Maracanã has reflected the broader transformations across the urban landscape, where accelerated gentrification is occurring en masse.

It is true that the World Cup and the Olympics bring extraordinary benefits, but they create profits for an international elite—the Brazilian construction industry, FIFA and the event sponsors—while the costs are socialized and borne by the Brazilian populace. FIFA paid no taxes in Brazil and committed one of the greatest heists in Brazilian history upon its citizenry.

JUNE 22, 2014. The World Cup is under way. Belgium and Russia are facing off in the opening round at Maracanã but I cannot get anywhere close to the stadium without a ticket. I ride the subway to Maracanã station and move through the crowds carrying a lot of weight: a large tripod, camera bag and a big pelican case with a GoPro-equiped drone. I am assessing vulnerabilities in security, an apparent specialty of mine, having one year before climbed a fence and snuck through two security gates to walk the parade floor at Rio's famous Sambodrome to film the main character from my previous film performing his most famous composition in Brazil's most prestigious Carnaval parade. Riding the success of this previous coup over the gatekeepers, I arrive confident at Maracanã, expecting I will again enjoy similar success.

After passing through one of the four police checkpoints, I am stopped at the second. My bullshit story about press credentials being held for me at the gate is falling on deaf ears, and so, while it appeared there was no way for me to access the stadium, the drone certainly could. I retreat into a safe space, still amidst the throngs of fans but in a small opening large enough to launch the drone and have it make a flight around the stadium entrance. While I captured some lovely shots the massive security forces are unimpressed, and I am soon accosted by a group of military police who explain that even the airspace belonged to FIFA. I am quickly encircled by another group of officers who are far more aggressive. They demand that I leave the premises immediately. I apologize, pack up, and hightail it for the subway, angry cops close behind.

I ride the subway one stop to the other side of the stadium and arrange for a friend living inside the security perimeter to come and meet me outside with his resident's pass. In his company, we easily pass through the police checkpoints, drone in tow. After some coaxing from my friend, I make my way up to his apartment rooftop. I am now immediately adjacent to the stadium, well inside the security perimeter, hiding from the police helicopters circling above. I wait for the game to end, intending to launch a flight as throngs of fans exit the stadium. The final whistle blows and up goes my drone, but not even 30 seconds pass before it is spotted and surrounded by two military police helicopters. I start to panic and crash-land the drone. I quickly retreat down the thin vertical tunnel I had used to access the rooftop. I hide in my friend's apartment, the roar of military helicopters hovering immediately above us in close proximity. I have found myself in many sketchy situations in Brazil but this bad scene was entirely self-created. The ever-present war of the helicopters rattles my nerves and is a sure indication that the poice have not forgotten about me. My friend assures me that the police will leave once the fans disperse. Sure enough that's what happens—a full two hours later, the longest two hours of my life. One more potential confrontation with the police has been evaded...for now.

JULY 13, 2014. The FIFA World Cup finals will be played at Maracanã today. Significantly, it is not the Brazilian squad but their arch rivals Argentina who will be facing off against Germany in the final, after the Brazilian team was annihilated 7-1 in the semi-final in what was the most embarrassing loss in the history of the World Cup. Nothing could be more apparent than FIFA's "state of exception" today. Rio is seeing one of the largest mobilizations of military and police forces since the end of the dictatorship. It isn't Brazilian citizens the police are here to protect. It's clear that they are protecting FIFA and the associated global capital interests. The police have been sent to the streets to brutally repress and censor any dissidents who might spoil the party.

And so it was in this context that I was savagely beaten by a group of military police. There was nothing particularly special about my case. I had witnessed many such unprovoked attacks by the police at protests before; however, on this occasion, it was a privileged "gringo" who had been attacked, and the story made international headlines. While the police have been beating, torturing and disappearing poor "favelados" for a long time, they had overstepped their duty and swung their batons at me, one of the international visitors they were tasked to protect. The fact that this relatively minor incident garnered so much international media attention is emblematic of precisely the inequalities Brazilians were protesting against in the streets that day: the transformation of the urban landscape in Rio and throughout Brazil to serve people like me, international tourists and capital, at the expense of the people who actually live here.

While I have no personal footage recording the moment of the attack as my memory card had just filled up and my GoPro stolen, the incident was partially captured by my team, who quickly gathered all of the citizen footage. They performed a frame-by-frame forensic analysis, identifying two of the aggressors and breaking the story online, publishing their profiles in close-up photos captured at earlier moments in the day. The offending military police were arrested within hours of breaking the story and have since been removed from active duty while they await trial. The arrests were truly extraordinary given the culture of absolute impunity amidst Brazilian police, and was surely a public relations move prompted by this major embarrassment coinciding with the World Cup finals. This marked an important moment: my own beating filmed by my collaborators turning their cameras back on me, citizen security provided by the citizens themselves. While it was a small victory for justice, for Brazilians, the incident only adds insult to injury. When a foreigner suffers a relatively minor attack, there is accountability, while summary executions and disappearances at the hands of the police continue on a regular basis with complete impunity.

As MOST OF the world watched the World Cup finals from the comfort of their homes, bars and restaurants in cities and towns across the globe, we should not forget the financial and social costs of creating this spectacle. Brazilians will be coping with the legacy of this event for years to come. While it's easy to dismiss my experience as an unfortunate incident perpetrated by a handful of "bad apples," we should take pause and consider the systemic context wherein the police are themselves victims of Brazil's oppressive political system under global capitalism. Most police are themselves favela dwellers who are poorly paid and trained. They are (in most cases) pursuing a career in policing due to lack of other opportunities, much like African-Americans in the United States, who are represented twice as much in the military as they are in the US population. This is not to dismiss the egregious violence perpetrated by a handful of the police, but amongst any mass harvest (the "thousands of new jobs created by the World Cup"), there are bound to be more than a few bad apples.

The police that were sent to the streets in Brazil for the World Cup and will be again in 2016 for the Olympics are not serving Brazilians. They are serving FIFA and the IOC, serving you, and protecting the status quo from the inevitable resentment that is going to boil up in host countries when the circus comes to town and no one bothers to consult or invite the people hosting the party. The problems run much deeper than the actions of a few bad apples: they are systemic and arise from the inherent dynamics of global capitalism. Events like the FIFA World Cup and the Olympic Games exemplify these dynamics. They are multi-billion-dollar commercial bonanzas that actively disenfranchise the majority to the benefit of the few. So much for the notion of fair play! As consumers of these global spectacles, we are all implicated in the story. In 2015, I intend to be back in Brazil documenting the next chapter of this tragic and infuriating narrative.

The Killing of Sammy Yatim

MARY ROGAN

JUST BEFORE MIDNIGHT on July 26, 2013, Sammy Yatim boarded a westbound Dundas streetcar and made his way to the back. He was wearing the standard teen trifecta of baseball cap, black T-shirt and jeans that hung loosely off his slight frame. Despite the late hour, the streetcar was filling up. It was a Friday night in the middle of the summer, and Toronto was hopping: Justin Bieber at the ACC, KISS at the Molson Amphitheatre, a beer festival at the CNE grounds and the Jays hosting the Houston Astros at the Dome.

Four young women got on around Spadina and found seats in the back, near Yatim. Soon after, he unzipped his fly and pulled out his penis. The other passengers heard a piercing scream and turned around to see one of the women jump out of her seat. Yatim had a stiletto switchblade and had tried to slash the woman's throat. The panic onboard was instantaneous. The crowd surged forward on the streetcar, some rushing down the steps to the back exit, most pushing toward the front to get as far away from Yatim as possible. Frantic passengers were screaming to get out as Yatim inched up the aisle toward them, but the doors wouldn't open on the moving streetcar and the steps quickly clogged with people. Yatim shouted, "Nobody get off the fucking streetcar." All the while, he had the knife outstretched in one hand and his penis in the other.

The streetcar driver saw the stampede behind him and stopped the car at Bellwoods Avenue, opening both sets of doors. Passengers pushed and stumbled their way out. Some landed hard on the pavement before scrambling away. Inside the streetcar, one more rider was backing up the aisle, dragging his bike in front of him like a shield as Yatim advanced with his eyes wide and his jaw clenched. By the time the passenger reached the front door, Yatim had switched gears and was telling everyone to get off the streetcar, so the passenger jumped out, bike in tow.

Behind Yatim, the car looked to be deserted. Suddenly, a male passenger who had been hiding between two seats popped his head up and crept over to the back doors. He stood there for several seconds, as if trying to guess whether Yatim was going to stay on the streetcar or go out the front, probably to avoid running straight into him. He decided to take his chances and ran out the back.

Then it was just Yatim and the driver, who'd waited until all the passengers were off before trying to make his exit. By this time, several people outside had phoned 911, including one of the women from the back of the streetcar, who was crying hysterically into her phone, saying, "A man tried to kill me." The police were seconds away. Yatim and the driver seemed to see the flashing lights through the front window at the same moment. The driver bolted just as Yatim lunged at him with the knife.

Yatim was alone at the front of the streetcar when Constable James Forcillo and his partner, the first cops on the scene, rushed to the open doorway. The only information Forcillo had when he arrived was that a man had tried to stab a girl on the streetcar. As the "roll-up" cop, Forcillo was the de facto officer in charge until a division sergeant got there. He pulled out his gun, a police-issue Glock 22 with hollow-point bullets, and stood roughly 12 feet away from the door, legs splayed, aiming squarely at Yatim. Like all Toronto police, Forcillo had been trained to take out his weapon only if he believed lethal force might be necessary. In other words, when a cop pulls his gun, it's never a bluff. He's prepared to use it.

"Drop the knife," Forcillo ordered.

"No. You're a fucking pussy," Yatim replied.

Forcillo asked his partner to radio for a taser to subdue Yatim. In Toronto, only division sergeants are allowed to carry tasers. Normally, there are two road sergeants for each shift, but that night there was only one on duty for 14 Division, which covers seven downtown neighbourhoods—the Annex, Kensington-Chinatown, Palmerston-Little Italy, Christie-Ossington, Trinity Bellwoods, South Parkdale and the waterfront. Forcillo's sergeant could have been in any one of them.

Over the cacophony of competing sirens as other officers arrived at the scene, Forcillo and two other cops shouted at Yatim half a dozen times to drop his weapon. Every time a cop barked, "Drop the knife," Yatim's answer was the same: "You're a fucking pussy."

Behind Forcillo, passengers were talking about what had just happened on the streetcar, some of them crying. It was Forcillo's job to contain the scene and make sure Yatim didn't get off the streetcar wielding a weapon. He could have reached Forcillo in one leap. If he jumped out into the crowd with his knife, Forcillo wouldn't have been able to use his gun without endangering bystanders. He warned Yatim, "If you take one more step in this direction, that's it for you, I'm telling you right now." Yatim turned away and stepped back into the interior of the streetcar, then appeared to make a decision. He turned to face Forcillo and took a step toward the exit. Another cop shouted "Drop the—" but didn't get to finish his sentence before Forcillo fired three quick shots. Yatim crumpled to the floor of the streetcar, still holding the knife. Cops were yelling "Drop it" when Forcillo squeezed off six more shots. He was the only officer to fire his gun. The cop standing on his right had his gun drawn but didn't fire. His partner, standing a few feet to his left, never took her gun out of her holster.

Almost a dozen cops raced over. Yatim was still moving, still clenching the knife, when the division sergeant arrived, darted through the front doors and tasered him. The crackle of the stun gun was unmistakable. Several more officers boarded the streetcar. One of them kicked the knife away from Yatim's hand, and it hurtled into the air, clattering against the streetcar window. Another began CPR. Forcillo, standing in the middle of the crush of cops clustered at the front door, abruptly wheeled away and stood alone for a few seconds. An officer walked over and put his hand on Forcillo's shoulder, leading him from the scene.

Police continued to do chest compressions on Yatim until the paramedics arrived and took over. He was pronounced dead at St. Michael's Hospital early in the morning of July 27.

Within an hour, a cellphone video was posted to YouTube and quickly went viral. It was reposted on Facebook and Twitter and led every newscast across the city. Toronto was transfixed by the last 90 seconds of Sammy Yatim's life. A city-wide consensus quickly formed: this 18-year-old didn't have to die. The police could have held their fire and waited for the taser. They could have tried to talk Yatim down instead of working him up, or shot the knife out of his hand, or used pepper spray. There had to be a non-lethal option available. And the question on everyone's mind was, what kind of cop shoots a troubled teenager nine times?

IN HIS SIX years on the force, James Forcillo had never fired his gun on the job until that night. He had drawn it before, during an arrest in Kensington Market, but managed to persuade two armed suspects to surrender without incident. Forcillo looks older than his 31 years. He has a square, heavyset build and a wary cast to his eyes. A second-generation Italian-Canadian, he spent his early childhood in Montreal, close to his mother's large family. His father worked in the textile industry, moving from job to job, with long stretches of money troubles in between. A job change brought the family to Toronto when Forcillo was 12. A few years after that, his father found work in California, and Forcillo and his mom split their time between Toronto and LA. When he was 18, he moved to California to live with his dad full-time, and his mother died of lung cancer shortly afterward. He enrolled in a criminal justice program, something that had interested him since high school, and graduated summa cum laude, but he wasn't able to work without a green card. His relationship with his father soured, and at age 20 he decided to come back to Toronto to pursue a career in policing.

Forcillo met his future wife, Irina, in 2003, when he rented the basement apartment in her parents' North York house. Like all cops, he's prohibited from talking about any case that's in front of the courts, including his own, but the rule doesn't apply to his wife, who agreed to be interviewed for this story. A manager in a financial services firm, Irina is a stylish woman, self-possessed and yet unexpectedly girlish when she smiles. She comes from a close-knit Ukrainian family that immigrated to Israel when she was seven and then to Canada when she was 15. You can still hear the mix of hard Russian consonants and Israeli inflections in her voice.

They were an unlikely couple—Forcillo is shy and quiet, and Irina is outgoing and boisterous—but her family quickly brought him into the fold. Irina was in the last year of her business degree at UofT, and Forcillo was following a well-worn path to the police force. He worked as a security guard and studied psychology at York. In 2006 he became a court officer, escorting prisoners to and from their cells and maintaining order in the courtroom. The following year, he and Irina were married, and the year after that, when Irina was pregnant with their first child, Forcillo got the call that he had been accepted into the police training program.

Forcillo's expectations didn't always match up to the reality. As a beat cop in the city's downtown core, his job wasn't glamorous. When he'd get home after a shift and Irina would push him to talk about his day, he'd say he didn't see the sense in telling her about crack houses or suicides or the drunk who puked in his car or performing CPR on a guy who died anyway. He loved his work—he'd tell Irina he couldn't imagine doing anything else—but he wasn't married to it. He was more likely to head straight home after a shift than go out for a beer with his fellow officers. Sometimes Irina would encourage him to socialize more, but he'd say that at the end of a shift he just wanted to put his hat on the wall and be a dad.

Anyone married to a cop worries. Before Irina met Forcillo, all she knew about police work was what she saw in movies. To try to reassure her, he told her a version of what most cops tell their spouses: "I could go my whole career and never have to use my gun. I hope I will never use my gun. And most likely I won't. So calm down."

Still, it was easy for Irina to fall down the rabbit hole of what-ifs. So she set some ground rules. First, she made him promise that no matter how busy he was at work, if she called him, he had to text her back, even just a one-liner to say he was okay, so she wouldn't lie awake at night picturing him sprawled on a sidewalk. And then something else: "I told him, 'You've got to promise me you're going to come home to me.' And he said, 'I promise you, if it's either me or someone else, it's going to be someone else. I'm going to come home to you.'"

AFTER SHOOTING YATIM, Forcillo was taken to 14 Division. Whenever an officer has been involved in the death or serious injury of a civilian, the Special Investigations Unit is immediately called in. Following standard SIU protocol, a sergeant took Forcillo's gun and cellphone, and segregated him from the other cops who'd been at the scene to prevent them from comparing stories and corrupting the investigation. He spent the next several hours in an interrogation room by himself, not permitted to leave unless chaperoned by another officer. The Toronto Police Association called the firm Brauti Thorning Zibarras, the union's go-to lawyers for high-profile police cases.

Peter Brauti looks more like an NHL enforcer than a top-shelf lawyer. He's well over six feet, with a shaved head and eyes that could drill a hole through cement. He was at his Muskoka cottage when he got a call from one of his associates. It was in the early hours of the morning, and the associate told his boss about the YouTube video. Brauti pulled it up on his phone and immediately understood how explosive this case was about to get.

Around the time Brauti was watching the video, Forcillo was allowed to make a phone call to his wife so that she wouldn't find out about the shooting on the news. When her phone rang at 2 a.m., she knew something terrible had happened: "He never calls me in the middle of the night. He said, 'Babe?' and I hear his voice and it's not his usual voice. It's a bit lower. 'There was a shooting. I was involved in a shooting. I'm okay. It was a good shoot.' I said, 'Is the other person okay?' And he said, 'No.' And I asked him, 'But it was a good shoot?' And he said, 'Yeah. But I gotta go.' And that's it. That was the call." After he hung up, Irina lay in bed, her heart thumping out of her chest, and waited for morning.

Her husband was allowed to leave 14 Division around 6 a.m. and was home by 7. He walked Irina through what had happened on the streetcar. Then he told her about the video, and they watched it together. "I was watching it and I wasn't concentrating on what's going on in the background. I was looking at my husband. You know, shooting. This chaos. The screaming and yelling." Irina didn't have time to think about what she'd just seen. She had to get to work and act as if it were just an ordinary day in front of her co-workers. But she understood the enormity of those 90 seconds: "He took a life. You're sitting in front of the person that you know very well, and now there's this additional layer. How often do you sit in front of a person who has taken another person's life?"

Two days after Yatim's death, almost a thousand people joined his mother, Sahar Bahadi, and 16-year-old sister, Sarah, at Yonge-Dundas Square to protest the police's use of excessive force. The group marched west on Dundas toward Bellwoods Avenue, carrying "Justice for Sammy!" signs, and chanting "Shame!" and "Think before you kill!" They stopped outside 52 Division and pushed toward the entranceway. Dozens of police officers held the crowd back and blocked the doors with their bicycles, while march organizers pleaded with protesters to stay calm. Forcillo's critics characterized the standoff as a typical example of the cops circling the wagons around one of their own. On the other side, police were feeling under siege, the actions of one cop tainting the reputation of the entire force.

In the days and weeks that followed, the story of Sammy Yatim's life took shape. He grew up in Aleppo, Syria, and came to Canada in 2008 to live with his father, Nabil Yatim, a management consultant, in Scarborough. His mother, a pediatrician and a devout Christian whose home in Syria was decorated with pictures of Jesus, stayed behind. When Yatim was killed, Bahadi was with relatives in Montreal, working on her immigration.

Yatim had attended Brebeuf College, an all-boys Catholic high school near Bayview and Steeles with a reputation for academic excellence (alumni include the social activist Marc Kielburger and the novelist Joseph Boyden). In his senior year, he transferred to an alternative school where he was reportedly hanging out with a new, tougher crowd and seemed less focussed on his education. After one in a series of arguments with his father, he had moved out of his home and was sleeping on a friend's couch.

Early news reports suggested he was mentally ill, but his family denied this, as did friends and former teachers, who characterized his behaviour on the night he was killed as anomalous. They described a sweet, gentle kid and said that whatever struggles he was having, at least up until that night, fell within the bounds of typical teenage drama.

The Yatim family hired Julian Falconer, a civil rights activist and the city's top lawyer for the families of people killed or seriously injured by the police. Falconer conducted his own investigation into the shooting, and, in February, filed a multimillion-dollar civil action against Forcillo and two other officers at the scene, as well as police Chief Bill Blair and the Toronto Police Services Board, alleging cruelty, excessive force and insufficient training. (At press time, no statement of defence had yet been filed.) Three official investigations were also launched in the wake of the shooting. Chief Blair called for an independent review to examine how police respond to emotionally disturbed people, and, in late July, the former Supreme Court Justice Frank Iacobucci released his sweeping report, which included 84 recommendations ranging from increased training to outfitting front-line cops with tasers and body cameras. The Ontario ombudsman, André Marin, opened an investigation into use-of-force guidelines, including de-escalation techniques. And Ontario's police watchdog—the Office of the Independent Police Review Director—launched its own review of use-of-force tactics involving people in crisis.

WHEN POLICE TALK about use of force, they're referring to the way they deploy all options at their disposal, from bare hands to pepper spray to batons to guns. For Toronto police, the training begins during the two-month program at the Ontario Police College in Aylmer and continues with mandatory refresher courses every year. The cornerstone of the college's teaching is the Use-of-Force Model, which is depicted as a wheel of concentric circles dictating how cops should respond to threatening situations. One circle lists the suspect's behaviour, moving clockwise from "cooperative" to "resistant" to "assaultive" to "serious bodily harm or death." The others outline an officer's response options, from simple observation to physical intervention (like tackling a suspect) to lethal force. The model is designed to address the fluid, unpredictable nature of police encounters, and it demands that cops continually assess and reassess a situation as it unfolds, making decisions on the fly.

When a police officer regards a situation as potentially life threatening, the only response option on the wheel is lethal force. An edged weapon confrontation (someone brandishing a knife or a pair of scissors) qualifies: faced with a knife, police officers will automatically take out their guns. They're trained to aim at a suspect's chest (which gives them the largest target and the best chance of immobilizing the person), and they're told to shoot until the threat is neutralized—that is, until the suspect can't continue the attack.

TPS officers are also taught to create distance between themselves and the person they're facing down, so there's enough time to respond if the suspect charges. This used to be called the 21-foot rule, but it's now referred to as a reactionary gap and generally considered to be closer to 30 feet. Like the Use-of-Force Model, a reactionary gap is specific to each situation. An officer considers how big, small, fast, slow, heavy or high a suspect is, among other factors, and decides how quickly he might close the gap.

At the police college, cadets are placed in a series of simulations at the Outdoor Village, an elaborate set that includes sidewalks, storefronts and sections of an apartment building. There is scaffolding in place above the scenes where class members can observe. In one scenario, a cadet stands in a courtyard with a bag over his head. The bag is removed and he sees a man sitting on a bench reading a book, about 20 feet away. The bag is put back on and then removed again. Now the man is running straight at him with a knife in his hand. Can the cadet pull out his gun in time? Does he have time to back up? The answer is almost always no. In another scenario, a cadet knocks on a door to respond to what he believes is a simple noise complaint. Instead, when the door opens, he's ambushed; a man with a fake knife charges at the cadet and tackles him to the ground, stabbing him multiple times. The knives in these simulations are electrically charged to deliver a jolt. The thinking is that electrical shocks drive home the point of the injuries a cop will sustain if he doesn't successfully subdue the assailant.

In another exercise, a cadet uses a red marker as a knife to attack a fellow cadet, who's wearing a white jumpsuit. The first cadet slashes and stabs away while the one in white does everything he can to prevent the marker from making contact. Despite his best efforts, the cadet in white is covered in red at the end of the exercise. An instructor then points out, based on the density of the ink and the location on the body, which of the red marks would constitute fatal wounds.

Cadets also learn communication strategies, roughly 12 hours over their two months at the academy. And officers are required to attend a three-day seminar every year that looks at the latest de-escalation techniques. But unlike what we see on police procedurals, a real cop won't strike up a heartfelt conversation with someone holding a lethal weapon. They're told to focus a suspect with clear, sharp commands—"Drop the knife"—in order to control the situation. Soft talk—"You seem upset; how can I help?"— the kind of communication that might put an unstable person at ease, can't happen until the suspect lets go of the weapon.

At a coroner's inquest into the police shootings of three mentally disturbed people, which wrapped up last February, Ron Hoffman, who trains new recruits in mental health issues, testified that police get extensive schooling in de-escalation techniques—both how to identify people in crisis and how to talk them down. When a suspect is threatening a cop with a sharp object, however, de-escalation isn't an option: "The officer is bound to act," he said.

The vast majority of arrests in Toronto—99 per cent—happen without use of force. And use-of-force incidents are on the decline. Our police are generally good at defusing incendiary situations, except when they come up against emotionally disturbed assailants. Like the three inquest subjects, Sammy Yatim was in distress—erratic and unpredictable, but not a hardened criminal. The TPS has Mobile Crisis Intervention Teams that partner mental health nurses with specially trained cops, but MCITs can only assist in confrontational situations once a suspect has been disarmed, and they're not on call after 11 p.m. Until we adopt a better model, Toronto's front-line cops will continue to make critical assessments in the blink of an eye under the worst possible circumstances.

Simulations and other training techniques can only do so much to prepare cadets for real-life encounters in the field. The best training for high-pressure situations happens on the job. The more experience cops have, the higher their tolerance for threat, and the less likely they are to shoot prematurely. Yet there's a shortage of veteran front-line cops in Toronto. The average street cop, like Forcillo, has been doing it for less than seven years. In a job that's increasingly stressful, messy, thankless and dangerous, the rewards just aren't high enough, so they're moving into specialized units or opting for desk jobs or training positions as early as possible in their careers. Police call the phenomenon "flight from the front."

ON JULY 30, three days after the shooting, Irina Forcillo was in her car when her best friend called in a panic. "They released his name," her friend said. "I'm looking at his face right now. It's on CP24."

Within hours, reporters descended on the Forcillos' North York home. Television vans and camera crews trying to get a picture of Forcillo and his family set up camp across the street. Journalists harassed the Forcillos' friends, relatives and neighbours for information. Irina was bombarded with media requests through Facebook and Twitter, and a reporter showed up at her mother's workplace. The Forcillos now have two daughters—Alexandra is five and Nicole is three—and it became impossible to get the kids in and out of the house safely, so they temporarily moved into Irina's parents' house nearby.

Irina shut down her social media accounts when threats against her husband started popping up everywhere. One anonymous person tweeted "We know where you are. Expect us." Police removed the most serious comments and continue to investigate some, but they keep reappearing online. "Fucking pig better go down for this or shit will hit the fan. I'm not fucking kidding pigs" and "It's way past time to have an INTERNATIONAL FRY PIG DAY! There was no reason on Earth for them to shoot that boy." Brauti received threatening emails, and a letter with a picture of the World Trade Center towers collapsing was sent to every member of his staff, suggesting that Forcillo's actions were equally heinous.

Forcillo was shocked by the deluge of online comments and news stories. He told Irina that he sometimes wondered if there was something else he could have done on that night. Mostly, she says, he felt betrayed: "I do something because nobody else wants to do it," he told her. "I do my job, and now the same people who call in the cops to help them and protect them are telling me what I did was awful."

Immediately after Yatim's death, Forcillo saw the department's psychologist, which is standard for officers involved in fatal shootings, and he continues to see a psychologist today. Peter Brauti, who couldn't discuss the specifics of Forcillo's case, talked to me in general terms about police shootings and said he has noticed a pattern. "Officers don't usually embrace counselling at the beginning, because it's a bit of a culture of, 'I did my job.' Or, 'I'm supposed to be a symbol of strength or confidence for the public.' But then after some time, you see them become more open to it because they realize, 'You know what? I'm not okay.'"

CANADA'S CRIMINAL CODE defines second-degree murder as the unplanned but intentional killing of another person without legal defence or justification. On August 19, just three weeks after the shooting, the SIU—which had interviewed streetcar passengers and other eyewitnesses, and had scrutinized all the cellphone recordings, surveillance images and security video—charged Forcillo with second-degree murder in the death of Sammy Yatim.

If Forcillo is convicted, he faces life in prison without the possibility of parole for at least ten years. It's an unusual charge, especially for a police officer in the line of duty. In fact, Forcillo is one of only three Ontario police officers to face a second-degree murder charge since the SIU was formed in 1990. One of them, Constable Randy Martin of York Regional Police, was acquitted in 2000 in the shooting death of 44-year-old Tony Romagnuolo during the attempted arrest of Romagnuolo's 17-year-old son. A fist fight had broken out on the front lawn of the Romagnuolos' home, and in the struggle Martin shot and killed the father.

The other case took four years to resolve. In 2010, David

Cavanagh, a Toronto Emergency Task Force officer, was charged in the death of 26-year-old Eric Osawe after a drug and weapons raid went horribly wrong. While Cavanagh and Osawe were struggling on the floor, Cavanagh's submachine gun accidentally discharged and shot Osawe in the back. The Crown, in conjunction with the SIU, originally charged Cavanagh with manslaughter, but the judge dismissed the case before it could go to trial. The Crown appealed, upping the charge to second-degree murder, and the case was dismissed for a second time—the judge ruled Osawe's death a "tragic but accidental confluence of circumstances that occurred in a high-pressure and high-risk situation." The Crown appealed again, but the case was dismissed for the third and final time this past April. Cavanagh saw a psychiatrist and was on medication for anxiety and insomnia for a time. He's still a cop but has not been in the field as an ETF officer since the shooting.

When Forcillo was charged, Cavanagh called him to offer support and suggested they meet for a coffee. "My first time meeting with him, I saw the look in his eyes," says Cavanagh, "an aloofness that was familiar to me—that 1,000-yard stare." Cavanagh is blunt about how devastated he was by his ordeal. At his first psychiatric appointment, he was so discombobulated he left the engine running in his parked car. "Nobody goes to work thinking *I'm going to kill somebody today.* To have something like this happen is unbelievable. You read about somebody facing the same charge—somebody who robbed a bank and killed a teller—and I'm facing the same legal consequences as this person even though I was executing my duty. Trying to make sense of something that doesn't make sense really causes the wheels to spin in your head."

When the charge against Forcillo was publicly announced, Yatim's sister tweeted "Good morning JUSTICE," and the city seemed to exhale a collective sigh of relief.

Forcillo was arrested at Brauti's office the next day and taken to a holding cell at Old City Hall. A few hours later, Brauti was in front of Justice Gary Trotter with his request for bail. Forcillo's in-laws posted his $510,000 bond, and he was released shortly afterward. The judge included a 9 p.m. house curfew among Forcillo's bail conditions.

There was nothing for him to do but wait. The Forcillos moved back into their house after the media frenzy died down, and he stayed home while Irina worked.

FORCILLO WAS REINSTATED to desk duty last February but is not permitted to carry a weapon or wear his uniform. His assignment to Crime Stoppers caused another flare of outrage across the city. A Facebook group calling itself Sammy's Fight Back for Justice issued a statement: "We are extremely disappointed that a police officer charged with second-degree murder of which there is ample video evidence is being allowed to return to duty."

Forcillo's preliminary hearing began in April and lasted four weeks. Prelims give both sides the chance to hear evidence that will be presented at the trial. As is now standard in most criminal cases, the judge, Richard LeDressay, issued a publication ban on any evidence presented at the pretrial. This is done to protect the jury pool from being tainted—an increasingly difficult task in high-profile cases when viral images flood the media.

In late July, the Crown added a charge of attempted murder, likely in case they're unable to convict on the murder charge. The trial itself won't happen for at least another year. The Crown will argue that Yatim's death was criminal, that Forcillo cannot justify the shooting. They will likely focus on alternative choices Forcillo could have made before firing his gun. He could have waited for the taser. He could have backed up to create more distance between himself and Yatim. He could have closed the streetcar doors. They will likely zero in on the fact that Forcillo was the only cop to fire, that he clearly interpreted the threat differently than the other officers at the scene. And undoubtedly they will hammer away at the shocking six shots he fired after his first three put Yatim on the streetcar floor as proof that he used excessive force.

On the other side, the defence will argue that every action Forcillo took was consistent with his training. That he had good reason to fear for his life and the lives of the people on the street. That he was charged with the responsibility of making a split-second decision in a chaotic situation, and that's exactly what he did. The jury will hear, among other things, about police training, rogue cops, troubled teenagers, illegal drugs, adrenalin dumps, sightlines, ballistics, biased media and cop culture. They'll have to sift through a mountain of evidence, including a 90-second video that can't possibly tell the whole story.

Happy Returns

Timothy Taylor

This March, I join my fellow citizens in the never-festive season of taxes—but what most people find familiar is actually quite novel to me. Since I quit my last real day job at the Toronto-Dominion Bank in 1991, you see, I have been an independent corporation. I have paid taxes, just not much on my personal income. That changed when I took a faculty position at the University of British Columbia last summer. For the first time in nearly twenty-five years, I started receiving an actual paycheque with deductions. March now has a weightier feel.

Weirdly, I relish it. Maybe it's just because Canadian politicians, whom I find myself despising almost universally at this moment, all tell me that I should resist paying taxes. If Harper says, more or less, "No tax is a good tax," and Trudeau and Mulcair have both ruled out tax increases for the middle class—as in *ever*—well, there must be something good about them.

That contrarian logic may lack robustness, but such is the state of our politics today. Virtually nobody campaigns on tax policy beyond saying taxes are bad. Here I find myself in agreement with a thoughtful new book of essays edited by Canadian civil servant and academic Alex Himelfarb and his son Jordan. *Tax Is Not a Four-Letter Word* attempts what could be among the hardest of hard sells: convincing people that they should be prepared to at least discuss taxes in the service of fairness, preservation of social programs, and ongoing economic health.

I might as well come clean here, at the top. From the standpoint of the conventional left-right spectrum (arguably defunct, more on that later), I'm not always on the same page as the Canadian Centre for Policy Alternatives, several of whose leading lights have contributed to the Himelfarbs' book. At the risk of over-disclosure, my high school yearbook recorded my then pet peeves as "poodles, math, and socialists," each of which I regret naming, though for different reasons and in varying degrees. However, I'm happy to concur with the CCPA in principle on this issue: we need taxation to become part of the agenda. My agreement with those experts, which defies the very idea of a political spectrum, draws attention to a critical point. Taxes represent more than just a political and economic discussion; they form part of a larger cultural one.

"Cut taxes not defense," read a sign that Alex Himelfarb once saw in the background of a Tea Party demonstration. Change "defense" to "education" or "health care," or "snowplowing," and you can Canadianize the sentiment and highlight the paradox in play: people have decoupled taxes from the services they receive. They no longer view taxes as payment but as punishment. It was not always this way, as UBC economist and tax expert Kevin Milligan points out; a complete sea change has occurred over thirty-odd years in how taxes are perceived by the public and used by government.

Himelfarb argues that it all began with economic neo-liberalism, as popularized by the Thatcher and Reagan

administrations and later by Brian Mulroney in Canada—
the principles we now all know: smaller government, lower taxes. I can testify to their seductive power, because I
was studying economics at the University of Alberta during those very years. I have a distinct memory of the Laffer Curve first being trotted out for a political purpose. In
a press photo, Stanford-trained economist Arthur Laffer
stands with President Reagan in front of a blackboard with
x and y axes plotting tax rates against revenue, the graph il-
lustrating that tax increases only generate higher revenues up
to a certain threshold, after which the relationship inverts.

Laffer did not put forward one magic, optimal tax rate.
He suggested a theory, uncontroversial really, in which the
taxable citizens, companies, and transactions in our economy resemble anything else in life on which we place demands—our knees, our spouses' patience—in that increasing demand only raises returns up to a point, after which
further increases result in your getting a lot less.

This was not implicitly an idea of the right, it should
be noted. Laffer said he got it from the legendary British
economist John Maynard Keynes, who is typically associated with the left, but this just shows that neutral concepts
can be weaponized in politics. Reagan used Laffer to justify generalized tax cutting, part of the neo-liberal economic
agenda to minimize government in favour of the market,
and the concept hit what can be seen in retrospect as a political sweet spot. Margaret Thatcher won in 1983, pulling
away with a 73 percent voter turnout. Ronald Reagan won
in 1984 with one of the highest popular votes in American
history. Meanwhile, in Canada that same year, Mulroney
was elected with over half of the popular vote and no other
party reaching fifty seats.

Neo-liberalism eased smoothly into the discourse because

people welcomed it there. Western economies were in stag-flation, and Canadian taxpayers were paying a quarter of every tax dollar toward interest on the national debt. In positing the antidote, which Himelfarb himself refers to as a "counter-revolution," neo-liberal economics overturned an understanding of the relationship between citizens and their countries that had existed since World War II.

"In the decades after the war, taxes were the hinge that connected us to a common purpose," Himelfarb says. "We were building a new society. Social and health policies came about during this time. Income inequality, which was huge before the war, was decreased. We created a middle class and progress both individual and collective was assumed."

We defined an optimistic, progressive Canada during those postwar years, in other words, and Himelfarb would have us believe that with the dawn of neo-liberal economics we began to dismantle it.

PART OF ME wants to dispute the charge. As a young economics student—during a time, let's say, when I hoped economics might explain everything—I was persuaded by the elegant simplicity and individualistic ethics of neo-liberal ideas. Yet I cannot deny the negative aspects of our situation today that derive from the three-decade project to get government out of our lives and rely as exclusively as possible on markets. Chief among these would be an endemic distrust and cynicism about political engagement. Admittedly, it is impossible to prove that big government, 1970s-style, would have avoided this outcome (even if we could have afforded it), but neo-liberal economics has proven to be an undertaking that eats itself on the occasion of its triumph. Tell people that government is evil for long enough, that it is wasteful and inefficient and obstructs our freedoms, and eventually they will believe you so thoroughly that it will impinge on the ability of you or anybody else to govern.

The economic legacies are perhaps even bigger concerns. While we are aggregately richer, the data is clear on the distribution of this greater wealth: real median incomes hover at around 1980 levels in Canada, and though low-income earners are probably no worse off than they were thirty years ago, the distance between them and the wealthy has grown vastly. Does income inequality matter? Well, for a long time conventional wisdom said it didn't; pursuing income equality via redistribution was thought to reduce overall economic efficiency. Still, it is notable that the International Monetary Fund disagreed recently, writing in a 2011 report that "equality appears to be an important ingredient in promoting and sustaining growth." As well, the research clearly shows that income inequality, to the extent that it contributes to poverty, has negative consequences on children and their futures.

In the end, intuition can probably guide us here. Sure, income inequality can serve as a motivator. It proves on one level that people can get rich under the right circumstances, and data does support the point that more poor people manage to become rich now than in, say, the eighteenth century. Eventually, though, income inequality contributes to a sense of futility, which neo-liberal economic thinking tends to exacerbate with its hard stance on how government and its redistributive efforts are a waste of time.

Here is where middle-income earners could contribute to the discourse, being neither fatalistically poor nor obliviously rich. Unfortunately, they are discouraged from doing so by the politics of our day, and by their own economic stagnation, which predisposes voters to reward politicians who offer tax breaks. Consider, suggests Milligan, that in the last federal election the Conservatives won on a suite of "boutique tax cuts"—for seniors, for working families, and so on—none of which meant much economically to either the government or the people receiving them, but all of which earned the Conservatives crucial votes. "A triumph of targeted political marketing," Milligan says. Of course, everybody knew what the transaction was all about, and faith in government for the common good fell still further from the dubious toward the ridiculous.

And so we arrive at the contemporary paradox, a "social trap" in Himelfarb's analysis. When pollsters call us, 72 percent of high-income earners will agree that, sure, we should probably pay more tax to narrow the income equality gap; 89 percent of us will agree that we should look at something like a millionaires' tax; and 60 percent will answer yes over the phone to whether or not there should be a carbon tax. Nevertheless, on election day, in the privacy of that voting booth, we will all do the same thing we did last time: vote for the government we think will cost us the least.

How telling is it that right after admitting to smoking crack, Toronto mayor Rob Ford pledged to get back to work "saving taxpayers' money," as if amid all of the chaos there could be no more ardent statement of his commitment to his constituency. It was neo-liberal economics in tragic, red-faced emblem: a tyrant denying his abuse and wagging his finger at the straw man of big government. Promising, promising, while the ground shakes and the house burns down around him.

IT IS A PRETTY compelling formulation, yet one of Himelfarb's own comments leads me to think that we require another dimension to describe the situation. Taxes were the hinge that connected us to a common purpose, he says, cutting to the heart of what they represent versus what they are, strictly speaking, collected to do. We pay taxes to build roads, to hire teachers and firefighters, to fund EI and income assistance. But we also pay to play, and the game in question is citizenship, membership, community. Surely nothing could highlight our vanishing willingness to meaningfully engage with one another in these ways than the experience of implementing the HST and carbon taxes in British Columbia, where Milligan says he encountered resistance, even among those who would receive full compensation.

"They would literally get a cheque every quarter reimbursing the taxes they had paid on coffee and gas," he says of people who remained bitterly resistant. "What ratio of reimbursement to taxes paid would earn support? Three to one? Eight to one?"

These were clearly not economic positions being staked; they were cultural statements about the willingness to contribute at all. Here is where, neo-liberal or Marxist or whatever we call ourselves, we should not be surprised. Citizenship, membership, and community are collective conceptions of the self, and our steady drift toward more individual self-conceptions has been underway for far longer than neo-liberal economics, and in ways that have nothing to do with the economy.

Viewed through the widest lens, we are in the late stages of what philosopher Charles Taylor has called "the great disembedding," a process whereby we increasingly define ourselves independently of formal obligation to any matrix or hierarchy. Perhaps the writer who speaks most emphatically to this dynamic is Alexis de Tocqueville. In his nineteenth-century book *Democracy in America*, he directly addresses how these impulses played out in the North American context. He observed Americans to have a belief in "indefinite perfectibility," which arose from their sense of equality. However, he also observed that in a society where all are equal and autonomous and endowed with a belief in self-improvement, we inevitably become less and less able to see ourselves as part of a larger narrative, one that involves our fellow citizens, as well as ancestors and descendants.

Tocqueville was not recommending a return to aristocracy, despite coming from Norman nobility himself. He recognized the potency of what was flourishing in America, with Canada not far behind as our links to the monarchy grew ever more symbolic: the will to seek individual freedom and attainment. What was alive in the souls of Americans and Canadians during that heady postwar run that Himelfarb understandably remembers with wistful fondness? A common purpose stimulated by the horrors of a recent war, yes, but also a surging, empowered individual, with newly acknowledged human rights and freedoms, and the seemingly boundless capacity for improving the world. *Indefinite perfectibility.* The 1960s and 1970s in particular, just before the neo-liberal counter-revolution, were a time of intense optimism and assertive individual flowering. Yet it would be a mistake not to connect the dots from the freed individual with inherent rights and value, to the me generation and onward, to such possibly perverted conclusions as "Greed is good," or even the hyperbolic Thatcherism "There is no such thing as society." The mistake is to ignore the Tocquevillian conundrum: that these impulses toward individual freedom and attainment also contain the seed of a selfishness that isolates and confines us, cutting us off from one another and from generations past and future.

In the earliest years of the neo-liberal counter-revolution, that selfishness may have seemed like the necessary fuel to power us out of economic malaise. Perhaps at that moment in history, a set of economic ideas was allowed to hijack the boat on which social justice might have otherwise sailed, but the evolution was not simply a shift from left to right. The culture as a whole was on the move across social as well as economic dimensions. Around the time that the Laffer Curve was first dusted off for political use, an epic hyper-liberalizing of both the self and the economy was underway, both born of the same impulse for freedom.

MAYBE HAVING A child has shaped me here in a way that my economics and business education could not have anticipated, linking me to something intergenerational, making concrete the idea of obligation, causing Tocqueville to resonate. Almost certainly, my time in the Canadian Forces had an effect, acquainting me (perhaps temporarily, but unforgettably) with how the civilian values of individual freedom and attainment both repudiate and yet paradoxically depend on the core military values of duty and sacrifice. You can't have the former without the latter, as World War II proved to Alex Himelfarb's generation.

Therefore, it would seem like an easy bit of reductionism to now blame Wall Street for everything (or poodles, or socialists), and what is easy is rarely best. An urgency exists here, I would argue, as we face something like a Tragedy of the Commons 2.0. Just as, in the original version, cattle farmers were observed to over-graze a shared field while sustainably using their private plots, we are failing to sustain a resource over which we no longer feel any obligation, that part of ourselves that was once embedded in citizenship, membership, and community. What is common among us—the environment, the education of our kids, just treatment for all citizens, the very idea of being Canadian—finds itself starved of investment. The damage, meanwhile, is there to measure: income inequality, a stagnant middle class, mounting distrust of leadership, and a corrosive, cynical political machinery that now competes for votes in a manner that is only semantically different from buying them.

We are good at individual rights and freedoms. We're not so hot at duty and sacrifice. And that is not simply because of neo-liberal economics. It is because Tocqueville was right 100 years before Arthur Laffer was born.

Unfortunately, we can't look to the past for solutions, because at no point in history have we been the people we are today. We can't devolve socially and re-embed into constraining hierarchies, and we shouldn't want to. Justin Trudeau's admiration of China's "basic dictatorship" is execrable on that level. Likewise the mayor of Vancouver, Gregor Robertson, for praising China's ability to quickly implement environmental policies with the comment "You can question how worthwhile democracy is in a lot of countries right now."

Trudeau and Robertson may question it, but we shouldn't. Instead, we should urgently commit to thinking about how free, autonomous individuals can yet reconstruct the common good, such that citizens feel a genuine obligation to it, and that will entail putting taxes back on the agenda. We need to pay, but we also need to be ready to play.

The good news is that this is already happening, in a scattered way. The Himelfarbs have released their book. Susan Holt of the New Brunswick Business Council has recently called for the province to increase HST and corporate income taxes to help reduce the deficit. Last September,

Missouri Governor Jay Nixon vetoed a piece of tax-cutting legislation in his state that he argued would harm schools and mental health services. In California, Proposition 30 passed last November, permitting new taxes to fund education. Meanwhile, over at the Patriotic Millionaires website, you can find 100-plus people earning over $1 million a year who join billionaire Warren Buffett in calling for President Barack Obama to increase taxes on the rich, including themselves. Which returns us to obligation. None of this works if we don't figure out how to feel the debt that Alexis de Tocqueville predicted we would struggle to feel.

"He willingly sets himself duties towards both [generations before and after]...and he frequently comes to sacrifice his personal pleasures to these beings who no longer exist or do not yet exist." That's Tocqueville on the citizen under aristocracy, something we might consider trying to duplicate using our necessarily more individualistic motivations. It may well seem like a stretch—a cultural change, an awakened sense of duty almost certainly reliant on a political leadership now non-existent—but then, nobody said this indefinite perfectibility business would be easy.

Can't Lit

Darryl Whetter

IT'S HARD TO find a Canadian visual arts grad ignorant of a technical term like negative space, but it's very easy to find a Canadian creative writing grad ignorant of, say, free indirect style or nested narration or unreliable narrators. For decades in Canada, university educations in the visual arts and music have been crucial to the careers and the creativity of artists and classical musicians. With UBC celebrating the fiftieth anniversary of its creative writing [CW] program, writing workshops in Canada are hardly new. Nonetheless, a Canadian writing education is distinct from its cousins in painting and music in at least two ways. Those latter programs have not recently experienced exponential growth in enrollment, and Canadian CW pedagogy remains, despite its institutional expansion and endorsement, wildly scattershot from program to program and even instructor to instructor. Pursue a Canadian BFA in visual arts, and you're sure to study colour theory. Pursue a writing undergrad in Canada and you're sure to study—well, there will be words, and, probably, characters.

Twenty years ago, Canadian visual artists studied their craft at university, but writers often didn't. Eighties-educated writers like Douglas Copland, Lisa Moore and Margaret Christakos actually majored in visual arts, not writing.

Now, graduate writing programs offer mentoring and peer critique (at a time when book editors are too busy marketing) as well as exposure to visiting authors, experience on literary journals and financial assistance. When Canada has more full-time Canadian artists (140,000) than autoworkers (135,000), we're long past delusions about writers shivering in garrets and need to consider the various realities of what Mark McGurl rightly calls creative writing's "program era."

Canada's art historians and musicologists don't design and manage the education of our visual artists and composers, but English profs (who have rarely published books of poetry or fiction themselves) routinely control the education of our writers. These tweedy vampires do so with obvious costs to national and personal truth-telling. The number of graduate writing programs in Canada doubled within the last decade, yet various factors within the Canadian academy (not the internationally popular discipline of CW), find most Canadian writing programs more devoted to the head than the heart and managed, not coincidentally, by English departments. Our writing grads are much more likely to be versed in Elizabethan celibacy or Victorian diarists than what Faulkner so rightly describes as "the human heart in conflict with itself." I've taught writing for more than a decade at four Canadian universities and am worried that—with English professors predominantly calling the shots—few Canadian CW programs teach or even entertain core writerly skills like social-emotional intelligence, revealing, engaged and accurate dialogue, dramatic tension, comedy and, most notably, plot. The current practices of our writing programs and funding agencies generally ask writers to be scholars who simply drop the footnotes, while graduate CW education in the US, the UK and equally post-colonial Australia values the unique fusion of personal and cultural truth available to the creative writer and her reader.

During a two year stint as the coordinator of the creative writing program at Dalhousie University, I repeatedly noticed our national preference for a colonial ownership of creative writing by an English department. First and foremost, the CW program there has no permanent faculty. The cart of individual careerism was characteristically put before the horse of national literature in 2009-2010 when the Swedish Academy invited Dal English profs to nominate Canadian writers for the Nobel Prize in Literature. Save myself ("Go award Alice"), no other Dal English prof bothered to write a one-page nomination to recommend a Canadian writer for the Nobel Prize. Canadian English departments don't respect living Canadian writers, let alone writers who teach writing. However, in the majority of Canada's writing programs, crucial decisions like hiring, genre concentration, pre-requisite qualifications etc. are managed by English profs (many of whom are professionally anglophilic Canadians). The bouncer's role that Canadian English departments continue to play with the very students and studies that could revitalize them suggests that far too many of our gatekeepers of writerly education have replaced a love of literary wisdom with the lesser love of being well-paid literature professors.

Unchecked discipline hostility appears to be one reason Canadian universities have not responded to the frankly insistent market for more Canadian CW PhD programs, of which Canada only counts two—at the University of Calgary and, *en français,* at Université Laval—while Australia counts more than 20. In *Harper's*, American author and semi-reluctant writing professor Lynn Freed refers to graduate creative writing programs as "the cash cow" of the humanities. As the website of the US-based Association of Writers and Writing Programs says "creative writing classes have become among the most popular classes in the humanities." Amazingly (and to national costs), Canadian humanities programs are uninterested in this cash cow. The trade secret for becoming an English prof in Canada is simple (though regrettably homogenous): do your PhD at the University of Toronto. The faculty pages of various Canadian Departments of English find the University of Toronto supplying more profs than any other single school. With one firm dominating the supply of Canadian English departments, other Canadian English PhD programs biannually agonize over one central question: how can we attract more and better doctoral students? I've heard laughably stop-gap solutions from profs who won't recognize that they need to change their product, not their marketing: *if we phone applicants, if we blog about the program, if only we had a better poster. Twitter!!* English professors, not student demand or even national funding, retard the conception and growth of Canada's doctoral research in creative writing.

With the federal dollars available to young Canadian writers shrinking, and our small presses either closing or contracting a finite number of books two or three years into the future, graduate writing programs offer junior writers crucial development time, space and money. The Social Sciences and Humanities Research Council of Canada is theoretically just as willing to fund a PhD thesis that is a Canadian novel instead of a disquisition about a Canadian novel, yet rarely fulfills this promise. Instead, crucial state institutions like SSHRC prefer a junior writer's scholarly potential, not her creative output. In *Muriella Pent*, Russell Smith's satire of the culture of culture, an application form for a Toronto artistic residency overtly states "DO NOT ATTACH A WRITING SAMPLE." This preference for explanations over art is funny in Canadian satire yet sad in public policy. The very real SSHRC does fund masters and PhD students (including CW students), yet its application similarly forbids a writing sample. SSHRC applicants submit a bibliography, but not their own writing. *Come, come, Ms. O'Keefe. Put these canvases aside and tell us who you're going to paint like.*

SSHRC could be a significant patron of CanLit. In 2008-2009, it doled out more than $300-million in grants and fellowships to graduate students, faculty, institutions and research projects, yet very little of that money went to storytellers and their traffic in social-emotional intelligence. The searchable awards database at the SSHRC site finds fewer than five fiction projects out of 121 projects in its Research/Creation Grants in the Fine Arts program for faculty. Projects in this formerly biennial half-program for artists have budgets as large as $95,000. Write about complex, vibrant characters, write like Alice Munro or Mordecai Richler, and you're not likely to win a SSHRC grant. Nano-splice language poetry into genes, wire the project to maybe record trace movements and put it on the Web, and SSHRC opens the coffers. Not funding stories means not funding characters and, arguably, emotions and the inner life.

Our national preference for argumentation and citation over emotion in CW pedagogy is further manifest in the oral thesis "defences" required in Canada's half-English writing MAs. The title and ritual of a "defence" suggest that a candidate can argue the merit of her collection of poems or stories instead of simply presenting stories or poems that are their own argument. At Columbia University, the largest and arguably most influential Master's of Fine Arts program in creative writing in the United States, a thesis passes or fails exclusively as a written document. If it passes, the committee then meets with the student at a "thesis conference" to discuss strengths and challenges. Canadian thesis "defences" are a clear hangover from the aped scientism of New Criticism (the zombie engine of English). In *The Program Era: Postwar Fiction and the Rise of Creative Writing*, Mark McGurl warns, "with its penchant for specialized vocabularies and familiarity with the less-travelled regions of the library, literary scholarship is at least partly in sync with the scientism of its wider institutional environment, the research university. Creative writing, by contrast, might seem to have no ties at all to the pursuit of positive knowledge. It is, rather, an experiment—but more accurately, an exercise—in subjectivity." Canada's institutional fear of the inner life wants arguments, not poems, and rarely aesthetic arguments at that. English in Canada remains hostile or indifferent to evaluative criticism. CanLit scholars are notorious for assigning books that are supposedly influential, not good (from *As for Me and My House* to *The Book of Negroes*).

The political fallout of Canada's creative writing hostage-taking extends beyond where and what is studied by whom and includes, perhaps most significantly, what is written. The academic preference for arguments over art-making risks a hyper-rational ghettoization of graduate creative writing material. For almost half a century Susan Sontag's essay "Against Interpretation" has proposed that "in place of a hermeneutics we need an erotics of art"; yet we keep steeping our writing students in hermeneutics, not aesthetics, focussing on buzz terms like rhizomes and palimpsests. To its credit, the University of New Brunswick's annual

Poetry Weekend invites its current creative writing students to read poems alongside published faculty and alumni. Notably, though, those students always invoke Jacques Derrida when reading their poems. Contemporary musical acts like The National and Iron & Wine (or Canada's Field Assembly) are known for their moving lyrics; none of them cite music scholars while they sing. When university writing programs deny emotion, novice writers easily succumb to affectedly marginal voices to recover it. For example, university-trained (American) writer Sandra Cisneros states overtly that when she wrote her breakthrough novel *The House on Mango Street* she consciously used "a child's voice, a girl's voice" as an explicitly "anti-academic voice." The marginalization of emotional complexity within so-called humanities disciplines can additionally distance the marginal voices many profs claim to serve (as when women write as girls).

Canada's disregard for emotional complexity creates a creative writing pedagogy that denies students literature's fundamental work with empathy. Scottish writer Andrew O'Hagan's novel *Be Near Me* (too intimate to be a Canadian title) has the best, and shortest, definition of education I've ever read: "managed revelation." Too often in Canada, a creative writing education involves conscripted decorum or endless reading lists from some elsewhere (whether it be England, the past, or the developing world) instead of "managed revelation." Days after 9/11, Ian McEwan published an article in the *Guardian* that hinged on literature's stimulation of empathy: "Imagining what it is like to be someone other than yourself is at the core of our humanity. It is the essence of compassion, and it is the beginning of morality." Aesthetic theoreticians and cognitive psychologists recognize the ways in which literature, especially narrative literature, allows us to expand our minds by thinking like others. In a section of his *The Art Instinct: Beauty, Pleasure and Human Evolution* called "The Uses of Fiction," Denis Dutton concludes: "Fiction provides us...with templates, mental maps for emotional life."

A national creative writing education that privileges literary analysis over literary production shuns interpersonal intelligence. One can hear the trendy phrase "rhizomatic poetics"—a term popularized by Deleuzians, that signifies the connection between two points without the burden of beginnings or endings—in any Canadian university English department (including those that offer creative writing); one rarely hears the word "empathy" or, in the context of empathy, the excitement that attends to rhizomatism. We adore the fragmentary but disparage feelings. In *Emotional Intelligence: Why It Can Matter More Than IQ*, Daniel Goleman rightly called social-emotional intelligence "a meta-ability, determining how well we can use whatever other skills we have, including raw intellect." In a land of methodology, thesis defences, bibliographies and Kenneth Goldsmith's institutionally celebrated "uncreative writing," the crucial meta-ability of emotional intelligence fostered by literature is not meeting its maximum audience. Who would decree that engineers should never actually build a bridge? Canadian English professors.

Story schools tell stories, and ours isn't very flattering. Without significant overhaul, the ballooning writing programs that could save CanLit from its yarns about yesteryear or saccharine imagistic somethings are simply going to waste more of our money and hope. Good writing educations can be found here, but they're too scattershot. I learned far more about writing, both fiction and poetry, in one full-year undergraduate acting class than I did in countless undergraduate and graduate classes devoted to faddish, B-grade literature or nothing more than professorial whim. Our students come to university with almost no respectful attention given to the creative arts, and when they arrive multiple factors show them that writing about novels is much more important than writing novels. Even when the production of literature is taught, it is almost always a marginal discipline, merely an indulgence from the colonizer (e.g., an English Department). A lack of respect breeds a lack of rigour. As a university discipline, creative writing should be a thinking and communication tool, and it deserves a place at every Canadian institute of higher learning.

Unacceptably, however, writing in Canada is managed (and sometimes even taught) by professors who have never published creative writing or have not published it in decades. Not even Canada would short-change its music or fine arts students in this way, yet we'll appoint unqualified English professors to direct or even teach story writing. The Association of Writers and Writing Programs knows: "in addition to advancing the art of literature, creative writing workshops exercise and strengthen the resourcefulness of the human will, and it is the exercise of will not over others, but for others, as stories and poems are made as gifts for readers and listeners." Canadian university after university in province after province has created a writing education that cheats its paying students of what Henry James calls the "great generosities" of literature and social-emotional intelligence.

Author Biographies

NADINE BACHAN was born in Trinidad and raised in the suburbs of Toronto. She now lives and writes in Vancouver, and is a recent graduate of the MFA program in Creative Writing at UBC.

TANYA BELLEHUMEUR-ALLATT's essays, poems and fiction have been published in several journals, including *Grain*, *EVENT* and *Prairie Fire*. She was nominated for a 2014 National Magazine Award as well as a Western Magazine Award. In 2015, she received a grant from the Canada Council for the Arts for *The Twelfth Year*, a book-length collection of essays. "Beirut Bombing," from that collection, was shortlisted for *EVENT* Magazine's Creative Non-Fiction award. She was a finalist in the 2015 Writers' Union of Canada contest. She lives in North Hatley, Quebec, with her family.

EVE CORBEL is a writer, illustrator, cartoonist, mom and grandma who lives in Vancouver. Her writing and artwork have been published in numerous anthologies, including *Bad Jobs, Exact Fare Only* and *Guests in Your Garden*; and periodicals, including *Geist, Grain, Makara* and *one cool word*. She is the recipient of an Alcuin Design Award and an Award of Excellence in Innovative Defiance.

ADAM GOPNIK has been contributing to *The New Yorker* since 1986. His books include *Paris to the Moon*, *The King in the Window*, *Through the Children's Gate: A Home in New York*, and *The Table Comes First: Family, France, and the Meaning of Food*. Gopnik has three National Magazine awards, for essays and for criticism, and also the George Polk Award for Magazine Reporting. He delivered the CBC's Massey Lectures in 2011.

PAUL HAAVARDSRUD is an award-winning journalist who's worked for both of Canada's national newspapers and can often be heard talking about business in the afternoons on CBC Radio. His work as a ghostwriter includes Gordie Howe's autobiography, *Mr. Hockey: My Story*, which the *New York Times* called full of "charming storytelling." He lives in Calgary.

JESSAMYN HOPE is the author of the novel *Safekeeping*, which *The Globe and Mail* called "a complex, beautiful story about the inheritance of Jewish history". Her short fiction and memoirs have appeared in *PRISM International*, *Descant*, and *Ploughshares*, among other literary magazines. Born and raised in Montreal, she now lives in New York City, where she received her MFA in creative writing from Sarah Lawrence College.

GREG HUDSON has a degree in journalism from Ryerson University. His writing has appeared in *Flare, Canadian Business, Toronto Life, Elle Canada,* and once many years ago, on McSweeny's Internet Tendency. He is the Editor-in-Chief of *Sharp* where his writing most often appears these days.

KATHLEEN KENNEDY's work has appeared in *Room* magazine, *The Antigonish Review, Prairie Fire, Prairie Journal* and *the Windsor Review*. She lives and writes in rural Ontario.

JOHN LORINC is a Toronto-based journalist who writes about urban affairs and business for numerous publications, including *The Walrus, The Globe and Mail, ROB Magazine*, and *The Toronto Star*. He is senior editor and politics columnist at *Spacing Magazine*. Lorinc is also the author of three books, including *The New City* (Penguin Canada, 2006), as well as co-editor of *The Ward: The Life and Loss of Toronto's First Immigrant Neighbourhood* (Coach House, 2015).

SINÉAD MULHERN lives in Toronto. When not writing, she can be found enjoying the city's beaches and west end restaurants. She mainly writes about women's issues, health and fitness. Her work has appeared in *This Magazine, Canadian Running, Reader's Digest* and others.

NAHEED MUSTAFA is an award-winning freelance broadcaster and writer. She's worked for a variety of media outlets including: CBC Radio, Radio Netherlands, and the BBC. Her writing has been published in *The Walrus, Foreign Policy*, the *Toronto Star*, and *Outpost Magazine*.

JASON O'HARA is a documentary filmmaker interested in themes of social and environmental justice. His MFA thesis film screened at festivals on four continents and won two awards. Since 2010, O'Hara has been in production on his first feature documentary, "State of Exception," about families facing forced evictions in Rio de Janeiro before the 2014 World Cup and the 2016 Olympics. O'Hara teaches documentary directing and production in Ryerson's documentary media MFA program.

MARY ROGAN is an award-winning magazine writer. Her work has appeared in a variety of publications, including *Toronto Life, Chatelaine, The Walrus, SEED, Esquire, GQ, The New York Times Magazine* and *The National Post*. She lives in Toronto.

TIMOTHY TAYLOR was born in Venezuela. He grew up near Horseshoe Bay BC and spent his teenage years in Edmonton. He has degrees from the University of Alberta and Queen's University. His novel, *Stanley Park*, was shortlisted for several awards including the Giller Prize. His other books include *Silent Cruise, Story House* and *The Blue Light Project*. He lives in Vancouver, BC with his wife and son.

DARRYL WHETTER has published five books including the pot-smuggling novel *Keeping Things Whole* and the bicycle odyssey *The Push & the Pull*. His debut collection of stories was a *Globe and Mail* Top 100 Book of 2003. A professor of creative writing and literature, he reviews books regularly for papers such as *The Globe and Mail* and *The Toronto Star*. A book of poems devoted to networked sexuality, *Search Box Bed*, is forthcoming in 2017. (www.darrylwhetter.ca).

Permission Acknowledgements

Grateful acknowledgment is made to the following for permission to reprint previously published material:

"Ol' Talk" appeared in *Maisonneuve* 52 © copyright 2014 by Nadine Bachan. Used with permission of author.

"Beirut Bombing" appeared in *EVENT* 43:2 © copyright 2014 by Tanya Bellehumeur-Allatt. Used with permission of author.

"Getting It Wrong" appeared in *Geist* 92 © copyright 2014 by Eve Corbel. Used with permission of author.

"Expos Nation" appeared in *The Walrus* (October 2014) © copyright 2014 by Adam Gopnik. Used with permission of author.

"Access Denied" appeared in *Alberta Views* (January 2014) © copyright 2014 by Paul Haavardsrud. Used with permission of author.

"The Reverse" appeared in *Prism* 52:4 © copyright 2014 by Jessamyn Hope. Used with permission of author.

Editor Biographies

CHRISTOPHER DODA is a poet, editor and critic living in Toronto. He is the author of two books of poetry, *Among Ruins* and *Aesthetics Lesson*. His award-winning nonfiction has appeared in journals across Canada and he was on the editorial board of Exile Editions for over ten years.

Award-winning writer DAVID LAYTON has had short fiction and articles published and anthologized in various literary journals, newspapers and magazines including *Penguin, Exile, The Daily Telegraph, Condé Nast Traveller*, and *The Globe and Mail*. He is the author of *Motion Sickness*, a memoir, which was shortlisted for the Trillium Award. His bestselling novel, *The Bird Factory* was published by McClelland & Stewart. His third book, *Kaufmann & Sons*, will be published by HarperCollins in May of 2016. David Layton is the course director for Backstage IFOA at Toronto's Harbourfront Centre.